In 25 years of using the services of various busines⦙ [...]
is the person who taught me the most. By using the principles in her book, my company functioned 100% better. I was able to build my business from 2 employees to 30. It was so profitable that I bought 3 houses including a multimillion dollar vacation home, and built my own office and warehouse. I sold the business and commercial building at age 62, am now retired, and spend my time traveling."

> —C. Schoonbaert,
> Direct Mailing Systems, Inc.

"Annabel was brought into our company to help us hit our goals and organize our growth track, which led us to staffing choices, a difficult part of running a business. With Annabel's help, and following the steps in her book, I was able to identify not just extremely motivated employees, but actual Superstars, the 5 percent! What a huge difference! I have now tripled my capacity to serve my large corporate roofing clients, in a much more positive and controlled environment. Annabel's book outlines precisely how to go about clarifying needs, identifying talent, and acquiring and retaining the Superstars needed to expand your company's sales and profits."

> —Mark Warren,
> Warren Construction and Roofing, Inc.

"Annabel is fiscally savvy with a good sense of business relations and customer service. She has profound knowledge and high level of expertise, and she has helped us achieve profitability. Her book details important skills needed to achieve success."

> —Duncan Reed,
> Reed Bros. Furniture, Inc.

How to Hire and Keep Top-Notch Employees

The Key to a Profitable Business

by Annabel Ayres

BUSINESS SUCCESS PRESS

All of the examples used in this book are true. In some cases, the names and some of the specifics have been changed in order to protect the privacy of the parties involved.

Book design by Marian Hartsough
Cover art by Dennis Ziemienski
Cover design by Ashley Geringer
Photo by Star Dewar

ISBN: 978-0-9889835-0-2
Printed in the United States of America

Business Success Press
P.O. Box 11224, Santa Rosa, CA 95406
707-585-3669
www.ayresnow.com

Table of Contents

About the Author

ANNABEL AYRES has been in the business world for more than 25 years. While in her twenties, she was the general manager of a corporate restaurant chain. She cofounded her own company while in her thirties and built it into an $8 million corporation in today's dollars. After she sold, people who knew she was successful started asking her for advice. She enjoyed helping others so much that she has been consulting full-time for more than 20 years.

Annabel currently practices in the greater San Francisco Bay Area in Sonoma County; however, she also maintains phone clients in other states. In the past she has consulted in San Francisco and other Bay Area counties, as well as in other states in person and by phone. Over the years she has guided clients, who started with small companies with one to three employees, through all of their growth stages to become multimillion-dollar corporations. Other clients have opted to stay much smaller, while increasing profits and time off for the owners. Others have built their businesses to profitability and then sold the business and retired on the profits. And still others got so good at delegating that they kept the business, reaped high annual salaries, and worked only a few hours per week.

Annabel's clients hail from all industries: service, manufacturing, retail, restaurant, and more. Her focus is usually on the business end: teaching the owners how to be profitable and, by delegation, how to work less.

How did she develop a deep knowledge of how to manage a happy staff? As she tells her clients, most people aren't naturally good at managing people, but it's a skill set that they can learn. However, Annabel is someone to whom management came easily. Over the years she has paid attention to exactly what works and what doesn't. She studied management and management case studies to broaden her learning. She studied personality systems, which give a deep insight into what motivates people and makes them happy. And for 20 years, she has been able to observe, through her clients, exactly what does and doesn't work.

Introduction

Most employers dream of having a team of efficient, cheerful employees who not only follow all of the manager's wishes, but also contribute their own input on how to improve operations and profitability. This dream team can hold down the fort while the owner is on a two-, three-, or four-week vacation, and eventually the owner can come in only a few hours a day, a few times a week, to make sure everything is running smoothly.

Well, guess what? A number of my clients have achieved just that! And furthermore, they didn't come by the formula naturally—they had to learn how to implement all of the strategies we will discuss in this book. Some of my clients have been happy to work reduced hours for years, while making a healthy profit. Others, having enhanced the value of their businesses by developing a turnkey operation, were happy to cash out by selling their companies for a good price. Others have sold their companies to the next generation, holding the reins less and less over time until they had confidence that the company would continue profitably.

Over the years I have worked with hundreds of business owners who have been willing to learn the secrets to a healthy, profitable company with happy long-term employees. **Your personal level of success will be determined by how willing you are to learn these techniques and to continue to practice them over time!**

I work with my clients on many issues other than hiring and retention—for example, finance, profitability, expansion, and marketing. But the reason I chose the subject of employee hiring and retention is because I have noticed over the years that employee management is the single biggest thing that makes employers unhappy. If you are striving for a harmonious workplace that benefits you, your employees, and society, you need to be willing to embrace and implement the strategies I address in this book.

I have taken note of the recurring issues that I hear about over and over from my clients. In reading the book, you can identify the ones that apply to you and learn how to fix them. For example, with regard to business owners who have the wrong person for the job, I often hear, "I hired this person because she turned up at the right time." Or, "I was desperate for help, so I hired my neighbor's nephew." Or, "She was experienced in her field, so I hired her." Or, "As soon as I hired him, I figured out he was a weekend alcoholic because he always called in sick on Monday mornings." Or, "It seems like a roll of the dice whether any given employee will work out." Or, "There just aren't any good employees out there who want to work for what I pay."

I also have often talked to business owners who feel stuck with the employees they have and who don't know how to either change their performance or get rid of them. You can give these employees the opportunity to improve by implementing all of the strategies in Part Two, the management section. Once you have put all of those things in place, it will become clear whether you need to let the person go or whether he or she is willing to do what it takes. There is also a chapter on how to let someone go.

I also decided to start with this subject because it is so essential to lifting the management burden off of the business owner so he or she can concentrate on other areas of the business, such as expansion and marketing. You will read real-life examples of how well the skills I'm teaching you will work. For example, you will learn about Jeanette, the video-store owner who was stressed, frustrated, and overworked. Once she implemented her checklists, she was freed up to expand her business by marketing and to increase cash-flow by managing her inventory better.

In this book, you will learn how to attract and keep great employees. This is an essential part of the recipe to fulfill your dream of having a profitable turnkey business.

Part One

How to Hire – Step by Step

.

Chapter 1

Getting Started

Hiring top-notch employees will pay off, but you must take your time and do it right. Various studies have shown that it costs a company a tremendous amount of money to hire the wrong person—not to mention wear and tear on the owner's psyche. So slow down, even if you're desperate for a new person. Get some temporary help or wait to fire someone until you have the right replacement.

Set your sights high and don't settle for less. Look for a person who is of the caliber to be promoted, if you have an organization with a ladder for promotions. Never forget that you're looking for an A+ employee.

You will be screening your applicants in batches, based on when you place the ad. If you don't get the right person in the first batch of applications, do as many batches as you have to. Each batch of applicants will take about one or two weeks to sort through and interview. So if you need to do three batches, it could take you six weeks to find someone excellent.

Even in a job market with lots of job seekers, you may need to do two or more batches. And even in a job market where it's hard to attract great employees, I always tell my clients that the right person is out there somewhere—it's just a matter of how hard you're willing to work to find him or her.

Have all of your hiring documents ready before you place the ad: list of qualities, job description, daily checklist, skills demo, and a well-written ad. Also have ready a regular job application and a "list of jobs" form. Find a local or online company you can use for background checks, if needed. Chapter 2 provides a checklist you can use to be sure you aren't missing a step and that you're doing the process in the right order.

Chapter 2

Your Hiring-Process Checklist

Following is your hiring-process checklist. Please refer to the appropriate sections in this chapter for more detail on each item.

1. Set your sights on an A+ employee and don't waver.
2. Create a list of qualities and skills.
3. Create a job description.
4. Create a daily checklist.
5. Create a skills test.
6. Create or duplicate the List of Jobs Form.
7. Write and post the ad.
8. Screen the resumes.
9. Create the phone-interview questions.
10. Do the phone interview.
11. Create, send, and screen the email interview questions and responses.
12. Email the list of jobs form.
13. Hold the in-person interviews and administer the skills tests.
14. Check references.
15. Do background checks and online checks.
16. Make a hiring decision.
17. Say yes or no to the applicant.

Yes, it's true—you need to write up several documents to hire this person. But don't let that scare you off! First, remember that you only have to write each one once, and then you'll have it done for the next time around. Second, most of these items don't take a terribly long time to accomplish. And third, if you just can't get them all done, do the ones you can and finish the rest either after you've hired or the next time you hire. However, in the true spirit of hiring the best, you really should take your time and have your expectations and documents written out before you hire.

Create a List of Qualities and Skills

The list of qualities and skills is the most important document you will create and the most important one to use as your guide while hiring. Most people make the mistake of screening applicants primarily for job skills and job experience. You must make sure you find someone with those things, of course. But what most people fail to look for and find are the personal qualities they wish to have in an applicant, such as reliability, promptness, cheerfulness, honesty, accuracy, and judgment. (See the sample list for more ideas.)

Create a document called "[Job Title] List of Qualities and Skills"—for example, "Bookkeeper List of Qualities and Skills." Then create a "Quality" heading and make a list of all the qualities you can think of that you're looking for. One thing my clients usually do is think of qualities they disliked in former employees, such as tardiness, and list the opposite quality, such as promptness, as one they are seeking.

When you're finished with your list (you should have at least 20 qualities listed), make another heading called "Skills" and write down the skills you're looking for. Those are easy, but be specific: Perhaps the applicant needs to be an intermediate-level forklift driver or an advanced QuickBooks user with four years of experience. Also, write down what skills are desirable but not mandatory.

Now that you have your list of qualities and skills needed, *use these as your guiding document for the rest of the process*. Include this very list in your Craigslist job description. Have it right in front of you when you do your phone interviews and your in-person interviews. Make copious notes during your interviews, right on the list, about things you noticed that might confirm or deny these qualities. For example, if one of the qualities you're looking for is good organizational skills, and you ask your applicant how he stays organized, and he tells you he has all of his DVDs organized by title and he color-codes his calendar for various types of events, that is a good thing to make note of. Believe me, after you've talked to a dozen people, you're likely to forget which person said that—or that *anyone* said that—so take notes.

Sample List of Qualities and Skills

Qualities: Prompt, reliable, cheerful, honest, can-do attitude, efficient, takes initiative, asks questions, good problem-solver, even-keeled, follows orders, helpful, gets along well with all kinds of people, excellent communicator, great judgment, open to constructive criticism, not defensive, detail-oriented, organized, accurate… (Add your own traits.)

Skills: Great with customers; great phone skills; great writing skills; intermediate Excel skills; intermediate QuickBooks skills; excellent general office skills; strong Windows skills, including ability to mange desktop files and perform routine desktop maintenance, such as running anti-virus software; basic office-equipment skills, such as printer and fax troubleshooting.

Never forget, you are looking for an A+ employee.

Create a Job Description

How can you truly communicate with a job seeker if you haven't taken the time to write down the job description? It doesn't have to be long, but it should be written.

First, choose the right job title. If you need to, review newspaper, Internet, or Craigslist ads to see what terminology is being used for the position you want to fill. I often find that small-business owners are tempted to hire an "office manager." This isn't really a job title. If you need an office person, you generally want to advertise for an administrative assistant, a bookkeeper, a customer service representative, or a combination of all three. Your job may be posted as Bookkeeper/ Customer Service, for example, or Administrative Assistant/Customer Service.

The next step is to decide who the employee's boss will be. If you have a small company with two owners, only one of you should be the employee's boss. List that owner's title as the supervisor.

Next, you should decide how many hours you want the employee to work and which hours will be best for the company. (Note that when you write up the daily checklist, you can use it to estimate the job hours needed.) *Ask for what you want*, not what you think the hypothetical employee will want. You will find someone out there who wants those hours.

Also, define what flexibility is required. If you are a retail store and the employee must be there from 9:00 to 1:00 three days a week with flexibility to work a fourth day, write that into the job description. If you are a seasonal company and you need help eight hours a day, five days a week in the summer, and then four hours a day, four days a week in the winter, write that into the job description. If you look long enough, you will find the right person. If you need the person on certain days at certain hours, insist on that. Think in advance about just how much flexibility you have in those hours.

Next, you will need to figure out the market rate for the position. Craigslist is a good source. Take your time and do the research. Large corporations are on a different pay scale from small businesses, so don't compare apples to oranges.

Next, you need to decide whether you will offer any benefits, such as medical coverage, vacations, and sick pay.

When it's time to write the actual job description, write down *responsibilities*, not *tasks*. Tasks will come later, when you create your daily checklist. For example, a responsibility is to keep one's workspace neat, clean, and organized at all times. A task is to empty the trash.

Sample Job Description

Company Name
Job Description

Title: Bookkeeper
Wage: $15–$18/hr
Hours: Three to four hours per day Monday through Friday, as needed
Benefits: Five major paid holidays per year, prorated
Supervisor: General manager

Essential duties and responsibilities include:

- Keeping bookkeeping up to date and accurate at all times in Quick-Books: AR, AP, check register, invoicing
- Maintaining all office paperwork systems and keeping all documents and spreadsheets accurate and updated at all times
- Providing the highest quality customer service when interacting with clients
- Creating the monthly financial statements by the 10th of each month, per the accountant's supervision
- Ensuring that all taxes are paid on time: payroll, corporate quarterlies, and annual property asset taxes
- Running payroll accurately and on time
- Following collections policies and making collections in a timely manner
- Keeping filing up to date and accurate
- Filling out all required checklists and other documents in a timely and accurate manner
- Keeping the office neat, clean, and organized at all times
- Maintaining the appropriate level of office supplies
- Performing other duties and tasks as requested
- Following all company policies, as well as all state, local, and federal laws

For written job descriptions, you can purchase software or hire an HR consultant to put in some extra verbiage describing which parts of the job are essential and what the physical requirements of the job are. This template is designed to make it easier to follow the law regarding people with disabilities. If the duties are essential, your employee *must* have the physical capacity to perform the job, but you also must make reasonable efforts as an employer to adapt your workplace to help your employees perform their duties. If you don't have the time and resources to add those items now, I suggest you start with the template I have here and add to it over time.

Never forget, you are looking for an A+ employee.

Create a Daily Checklist

Often my clients feel uncomfortable giving their employees checklists because they think it may come across as demeaning or as if they are treating the employees like children. On the contrary, checklists give employees direction, structure, and a feeling of accomplishment at the end of the day when everything is checked off. Many, many things aren't covered by checklists and will require employees' judgment and creativity. But if employees aren't instructed on how you want the everyday basics done, they'll spend their time reinventing the wheel and doing things differently from how you want them to be done.

In my many years of experience, I have found that the type of employee who doesn't like checklists is the employee who doesn't want to be held accountable. So, beware if you have an employee who resists them. Checklists are used more and more in many professional situations.

Checklists are a basic part of quality management. For information on how to make them work for you after your employee is hired, please refer to Part Two of this book.

The daily checklist is the most detailed and one of the most crucial tools for you to use to attract the best employee and to keep that person on track after hiring. Your daily checklist might take only a couple of hours to create. This is such a small time investment to get the results you want day after day. After you've created it, you simply need to consistently add to it, update it, and review it a little at a time, until it's a complete and polished list of all tasks required for the job. It's okay to start with a fairly rough draft, but if you do that, don't drop the ball as soon as your new person is hired. Pay attention and update the checklist continually. It is a constant work in progress because things change day to day, week to week, and month to month, and your checklist needs to reflect all of these changes.

Checklist Structure

Your goal is to have all of your procedures written up in a series of lists. Resist the impulse to print them out and put them in a binder! They will just get outdated and collect dust. Please note that I will use the term "daily checklist" for each employee's main checklist. I will use the term "procedural checklist" for all other checklists.

You will have a daily checklist for each job position, as well as a series of other step-by-step procedural checklists. You should refer to *all* of the procedural checklists somewhere on the daily checklist so they don't get forgotten. For example, the daily checklist for the bookkeeper position will have an item on it that says payroll must be done on a certain day each month, and that item will instruct the employee to print out the payroll procedural checklist and check it off while doing payroll. The daily checklist will note exactly where the employee can find that procedural checklist on the computer.

Keep all of your checklists in word-processing files and include in your daily checklists the procedural-checklist file locations so that your staff can find them.

Titles

You will amass a number of checklists over the years, so start out by naming them Daily Checklist - Bookkeeper, Daily Checklist - Warehouse Manager, and so on. This way, the filenames will all start with the words "Daily Checklist," and you can keep them in the Daily Checklist folder on your computer.

A word of caution: Just because you created a nice checklist, that doesn't mean it will be used properly. Right now, we're talking about using it as a hiring tool. Later, you will learn to actually administer the checklist so that it is used correctly.

Now that you have finished your daily checklist, you can use it as a tool to estimate how many hours you will need for the position. Maybe this is the first bookkeeper you have hired, or maybe the last one you had was very slow and inefficient. Here's how you can estimate the time needed. First, print out your new checklist. Then, on the left-hand side, where the check mark goes, enter how many minutes each task will take. Add the minutes up, and you will find out how much time will be needed to do the job.

If you're wondering whether to skip the daily checklist, don't! This is one of the most useful tools for both you and your employee. Here is a true story about the power of checklists.

The Video Store

Management Tools: Checklists and Promotion Path

Jeanette was the owner of a video store. When I first met her, she was stressed, overworked, and distressed by how poorly her store was being run by her employees. They weren't providing customer service up to her standards, and at the end of the day she would spend hours straightening up and organizing the videos—picking up the pieces that the employees had left undone.

The problem, in short, was poor performance by her employees, which resulted in poor customer service, which resulted in decreased sales.

The solution was twofold: 1) Designate a team leader for each shift, and 2) Implement a system of checklists so that operations would run smoothly, customers would get great service, and the owner would have extra time to implement a marketing plan that I helped her develop to bring in new customers.

Jeanette and I sat down together and used the checklist format described earlier to make two different checklists: one for the team leaders and one for the video-store associates. Each checklist covered items such as how to greet customers (smile, look customers in the eye, and say, "Hello, may I help you find something?"). The checklist also included items for how often to patrol the aisles to straighten cases and how often to clean the glass doors. It instructed employees to empty the trash and sweep before they clocked out, as well as to watch customers for shoplifting.

The team leader's checklist included items such as making sure the rest of the staff was using their checklists, supervising the video-store associates, and doing the drawer countdown at the end of the shift. Jeanette had told her employees verbally to do all of these things, but they just weren't getting done.

Because Jeanette's business had only two positions—team leader and video-store associate—she needed only two checklists. We completed these in a couple of hours, and she was ready to go. I gave Jeanette careful and specific instructions about how to implement them and turned her loose.

I met with Jeanette again a week later, and she was all smiles. She was exuberant that she didn't have to clean up after her employees anymore. She said they embraced the checklists beautifully, and everyone was happy. Jeanette noticed that her staff left each day feeling successful about checking off all of their items. The staff was also happy, because they knew the owner was now pleased with their work.

Jeanette's time was freed up after implementing the checklists, so we were able to create a marketing plan for her. Soon, she had more new customers coming in, and her customer-retention level was higher due to better customer service.

In the end, Jeanette had better profits, less stress, and more time off! For the first time, she felt confident about scheduling vacations, because she knew her team leaders would take responsibility and that her entire team was trained and performing to her standards.

Create a Skills Test

Take some time and really think about what you should put in a skills demo. If you're looking for an employee who will be working on a computer, have her use the computer programs she will be working with. Create tasks and see how well she can complete them. For example, have her write a letter to a customer and create a file to put it in. Or have her create an Excel worksheet using the level of skills she will need. Think of as many tasks as you can so that you know what you're getting. You will, of course, have discussed the prospective employee's level of skill in each of these areas during the interview.

If you're hiring for a very technical job, such as a machine operator or a skilled woodworker, I suggest an extra step. After the applicant has completed the regular skills test, invite the prospective employee to work a few shifts as a fill-in on a casual basis. This will give you a very noncommittal way to see what his skill levels are. If you have advertised for the position and the person knows you are looking, you can tell him that you're still screening applicants and you need some temporary help in the meantime. You may even want to come in for half a day on a Saturday and work with the applicant to get a good feel for his skills.

Before the applicant arrives, have your skills demo worked out and each step written down for yourself, with spaces where you can take notes. Then sit with the applicant, verbally tell her what to do, and watch carefully to see her competency. Write down notes at every step, even if you just jot down "good" or "great."

Don't be tempted to skip the skills test! You can determine so many things from a skills test. Is your applicant calm and careful or confident and fast? Sometimes quick people forget to go back and check for accuracy. Is your applicant daunted by something unfamiliar? Does he ask questions at the right time? How does he figure out how to do something in an unfamiliar setting?

Here is a story that will reinforce the importance of a skills test.

The Electrical-Contracting Company

A client who owned an electrical-contracting company was doing a great job of following the hiring checklist. I helped her create all of the forms in advance and design her skills test. She had found a fabulous applicant—glowing letters of recommendation, a super personality, and a need for the same hours and wages that were offered. The applicant said she loved using Access databases and was experienced with the software. However, when the owner asked her to design a simple database query, it was clear that she was an absolute beginner in that type of database use. It turned out that she could work within the confines of an already existing database but couldn't make any simple design changes. The applicant was so good that the owner considered hiring her anyway and training her to create database reports. However, she decided that the need was too extensive, so she hired someone else instead. To do so, she had to run two more ads and sort through two more batches of resumes, but she ended up with just the right person.

Purchase a Standard Job Application Form

Locate a standard job application from an office-supply store or the Internet. That way, you will be sure to get basic information, such as a social security number.

Create or Duplicate the List of Jobs Form

List of Jobs Form   Name_____

List *all* jobs for the past 10 years, plus any other relevant jobs. If there is a gap in dates, list the reason for it.

Start Date _____ End Date_____
Company Name _____ Job Title _____
Supervisor 1 Name _____ Supervisor 2 Name _____
Supervisor 1 Current Phone # _____ Supervisor 2 Current # _____
Reason for Leaving _____

Start Date _____ End Date_____
Company Name _____ Job Title _____
Supervisor 1 Name _____ Supervisor 2 Name _____
Supervisor 1 Current Phone # _____ Supervisor 2 Current # _____
Reason for Leaving _____

Start Date _____ End Date_____
Company Name _____ Job Title _____
Supervisor 1 Name _____ Supervisor 2 Name _____
Supervisor 1 Current Phone # _____ Supervisor 2 Current # _____
Reason for Leaving _____

Start Date _____ End Date_____
Company Name _____ Job Title _____
Supervisor 1 Name _____ Supervisor 2 Name _____
Supervisor 1 Current Phone # _____ Supervisor 2 Current # _____
Reason for Leaving _____

Start Date _____ End Date_____
Company Name _____ Job Title _____
Supervisor 1 Name _____ Supervisor 2 Name _____
Supervisor 1 Current Phone # _____ Supervisor 2 Current # _____
Reason for Leaving _____

Start Date _____ End Date_____

Company Name _____ Job Title _____

Supervisor 1 Name _____ Supervisor 2 Name _____

Supervisor 1 Current Phone # _____ Supervisor 2 Current # _____

Reason for Leaving _____

Start Date _____ End Date_____

Company Name _____ Job Title _____

Supervisor 1 Name _____ Supervisor 2 Name _____

Supervisor 1 Current Phone # _____ Supervisor 2 Current # _____

Reason for Leaving _____

Start Date _____ End Date_____

Company Name _____ Job Title _____

Supervisor 1 Name _____ Supervisor 2 Name _____

Supervisor 1 Current Phone # _____ Supervisor 2 Current # _____

Reason for Leaving _____

Start Date _____ End Date_____

Company Name _____ Job Title _____

Supervisor 1 Name _____ Supervisor 2 Name _____

Supervisor 1 Current Phone # _____ Supervisor 2 Current # _____

Reason for Leaving _____

Start Date _____ End Date_____

Company Name _____ Job Title _____

Supervisor 1 Name _____ Supervisor 2 Name _____

Supervisor 1 Current Phone # _____ Supervisor 2 Current # _____

Reason for Leaving _____

Start Date _____ End Date_____

Company Name _____ Job Title _____

Supervisor 1 Name _____ Supervisor 2 Name _____

Supervisor 1 Current Phone # _____ Supervisor 2 Current # _____

Reason for Leaving _____

Write and Post the Ad

Nowadays, most ads for small businesses are posted on Craigslist. For a modest amount, you can post a nice, long ad. The best places to advertise will vary depending on your region, but I suggest starting with Craigslist. If you're in a small community where most people read the local paper, that may be worth a try. For large corporations or for very specialized, skilled job positions, you may want to use a headhunter or other online service.

When you place an ad on Craigslist, the ad will stay posted for a long time, but as other ads get posted above it, your ad will become obsolete—usually in about a week or two. As I mentioned before, you will want to review your applicants in batches. So, post one ad, see how many resumes you get, review the whole batch, do the interviews, and then post another ad in a week or two if you haven't gotten enough great applicants. Even in a market with lots of people looking for work, my clients often have to run their ads twice. In a market with high demand for good employees, you may have to post your ad every week for three to six weeks—or maybe more.

Write the Ad

If you're posting the job in a Craigslist-designated region, consider putting the name of the town right after the job title. For example, Bookkeeper PT - Santa Rosa. This will help applicants know that the job is part time and also where it's located while they are scrolling through the listings.

Next, write a brief description of the job and the company. Include required skills and talk about company strengths. List the company website but make it clear that people must apply by email. If you don't want a current employee to know that you are replacing him, you can run a blind ad. In a blind ad, you leave out the website and have the inquiries emailed to you through Craigslist.

Here's a tip for getting a little more information about some of your applicants: Use a Gmail account as the destination for your Craigslist resumes. Google has a feature called Google+, which is similar to Facebook or LinkedIn, where users set up a profile with photos, postings, and personal information. If the applicant has set up her profile on Google+, you will be able to see her photo and other postings. Some photos are odd and amusing; I'm sure applicants weren't planning for a prospective employer to view them! Which reminds me: It's good to keep a sense of humor about screening resumes! I've recently been screening resumes for a client, and I chuckle every time I read a cover letter that claims a "vast" set of skills. Why are so many applicants getting the idea to use that word? They seem to be mostly twenty-somethings. That occasional chuckle helps lighten up the task of reviewing an otherwise somewhat depressing lineup of resumes from clueless job seekers.

Sample Ad

Here's a sample ad for an office position.

Bookkeeper/Customer Service/Administrative Assistant - Part Time - Santa Rosa

A Santa Rosa construction company seeks an experienced, professional office person. Must have minimum of three years' experience with QuickBooks, customer service, and administrative work. This is a small, two-person office. The person in this position will often have to work alone in the office, answering phones, keeping current on bookkeeping and other duties as requested, while the owner is often on the construction site. The company is fiscally sound, has an excellent reputation, and has been in business for approx. 25 years. The owner has excellent relations with customers and staff and expects a high standard of work from a self-motivated staff. www.constructioncompany.com. Please reply by sending a resume with pay history to the Craigslist response e-mail.

Job Description

Title: Bookkeeper/Customer Service/Administrative Assistant
Supervisor: Accounting Supervisor
Pay: $15–$19 per hour depending on experience
Hours: Flexibility required, between 10–20 hours per week.
Probable/approximate schedule will be M–F 8–12 May–Nov and MWF 8–11 Dec–April.

Essential Duties and Responsibilities Include:

- Keeping bookkeeping up to date and accurate at all times in QuickBooks and other documents and spreadsheets.
- Providing the highest level of customer service.
- Running occasional errands as requested.

- Meeting with accounting supervisor monthly to review bookkeeping and run reports. Creating the monthly financial statements by the 10th of each month, per the accounting supervisor's direction.
- Working with accounting supervisor to make sure all taxes are paid on time: payroll, corporate quarterlies, annual property asset taxes.
- Running payroll accurately and on time.
- Performing collections duties.
- Coordinating with crews regarding billing for extras and timecard issues.
- Making sure all documents are created and filed accurately.
- Filling out all required checklists and other documents in a timely and accurate manner.
- Keeping the office neat, clean, and organized at all times.
- Maintaining an appropriate level of office supplies.
- Administering a safety program.
- Communicating with the president in a timely manner to resolve any questions or concerns.
- Performing duties and tasks as requested.
- Following all company policies, as well as all state, local, and federal laws.

List of Required Qualities

- Honesty
- Great phone voice and customer-relations skills
- Able to work alone or with a team
- Good at juggling tasks/interruptions
- Can-do attitude
- Accurate
- Efficient

- Reliable
- Prompt
- Organized
- Takes initiative
- Good problem-solver
- Good judgment
- Even-keeled
- Follows orders
- Okay with seasonal stressful/hectic situations
- Good with numbers
- Likes to suggest improvements but asks for permission before making changes
- Attitude of making owner's job easier
- Good at collections, willing to collect from customers promptly
- Takes pride in work
- Not defensive—can admit mistakes and learn from them
- Excellent communication skills, including spelling

Skills and Qualifications
- Spanish is a plus
- Valid California driver's license and car for occasional work errands
- Intermediate to advanced QuickBooks skills: invoicing, AR, AP, payroll, job costing, check register
- Computer skills: Intermediate to advanced Excel skills required (ability to build and maintain spreadsheets); Word: Advanced skills in composing documents (letters, contracts, change orders, labels, mailers); Windows: Ability to manage desktop files and perform routine desktop maintenance, such as spyware and anti-virus tasks
- Office-equipment skills: basic printer and fax troubleshooting

Post the Ad

Posting an ad on Craigslist currently costs $75, and it's a real bargain. Remember to remove the ad once you've chosen an applicant, to avoid cluttering your inbox and wasting the time of unknowing job applicants. Their task of finding a job is difficult enough without creating cover letters for jobs that are no longer open.

Screen the Resumes

Never forget, you're looking for an A+ employee.

My suggestion regarding screening resumes is to act quickly and screen heavily. Create folders for "Best" and "Good" resumes. Print out the best resumes, review them, and make notes. Here's how I screen carefully:

1. Next to each job on an applicant's resume, write down the length of time they stayed and whether there was a gap in employment. Eliminate the "job hoppers" who move on after a year or two. Make notes about gaps in preparation for your phone interview.

2. Carefully evaluate the specific time the applicant has spent using the specific skills you desire. If you're looking for three years of QuickBooks experience, but the applicant has 20 years of experience with various other bookkeeping software programs and only one year of QuickBooks, she is probably still a strong candidate. If the applicant has three years of QuickBooks experience but not doing all of the tasks you require, it may not be a good match. Don't make the mistake of hiring someone who hasn't performed the work you require for the required amount of time! In general, you want a proven history illustrating that your applicant actually likes and wants to do the type of work you require. Look for both aptitude *and* experience.

3. Watch out for people who are in deep change or crisis: newly relocated from another area, newly divorced, having financial problems, and so on. Please note to take care regarding discrimination laws. I suppose the law *could* be stretched to cover this type of situation.

4. Pay attention to students. What are they studying and when will they graduate? If a student is studying to be a police officer and will graduate in a year, it's not a good idea to hire him as your permanent bookkeeper. On the other hand, if an applicant is studying to be a teacher, will graduate in four years, and is applying for a wait-staff job in a restaurant, this could be a fine match.

5. Avoid people who are taking a step down or a step up in pay. Avoid overqualified people. (See #2 about proven history above.)

6. Beware of fake letters of reference. Always call the business and speak to the person who supposedly wrote the letter. It's easy for an employee to steal some letterhead and create a letter. Yes, it does happen.

7. Screen all of your resumes—daily, if you can—and select the applicants who are stable and who have a good history of doing the same type of work. Time is of the essence if you find a really good candidate. However, if you find a good candidate and wish to go to the next stage of the phone interview, do *not* stop screening the other resumes. You will generally need a pool of two to six people who look excellent on paper. Just don't try to find all six in the first batch by lowering your standards!

Create the Phone-Interview Questions

Prepare for your interview by creating a list of questions before you make the call. Print out the list, leaving plenty of space to take notes as you talk. Include items you will be judging, such as phone voice and phone presentation, especially if the person will be on the phone with customers, vendors, or other staff.

Here are some sample questions:

- Tell me about your availability. What hours will work for you? What are your ideal hours?
- How will you be able to work with the flexible hours we require?
- How much do you need to earn?
- Can you take on more hours if we get busier?
- How much did you make at each of your previous jobs? What are your pay needs now?
- How do you feel about working in a small office? (You can tailor this question for any other specific environment or requirement you might have.) Have you done so in the past?
- For which of the jobs listed did you use a CAD program? Which program was it? (Again, you can tailor this question for your specific software-knowledge requirements.)
- Why did you leave this job? (Ask about each individual job.)
- When can you start?

Be sure to write down specific questions that come up when reading the applicant's resume—for example, Why was there a time gap of four years between two jobs?

Include any other questions you can use to make sure the person has the basic skills you need.

Do the Phone Interview

In the phone interview, it's important to make a judgment about whether the applicant will be happy with the pay. If the economy is booming, applicants won't want to take a decrease in pay; in fact, you may have to offer more than they were making before. If the economy is weak, it's sometimes a good idea to hire someone even if he is taking a significant drop in pay. For example, I just screened an applicant (for a client) who had worked for 20 years at a very unique, profitable company and was making more than $40 per hour as an administrative assistant. She was well aware that the most she could hope for in her area and in the current economy was about $18 per hour. She had been looking for a job for five months and was reconciled to lower pay. She also had adjusted to living on only her husband's salary for a while, and she knew she could afford to live on the amount that was offered. I was very careful to get all of this information during the phone interview so I wouldn't waste the client's time interviewing someone whose needs and expectations didn't fit the pay being offered.

During the phone interview, you should also explore how the applicant's life will fit with the job hours. Start by asking the person what his ideal hours would be. Then compare those to the hours offered for the position. Explore the applicant's personal needs. For example, the person I mentioned a moment ago has three kids and has to drive one of them to and from school. We determined that she would have enough time to get to her child's school after work if she left at the 2:00 ending time listed on the job posting. The employer can decide before the in-person interview whether he needs more flexibility than that. Perhaps UPS comes every day at 2:30, and he needs her to be available for an extra half hour several times a week. The point is, be sure to ask whether the applicant needs any other type of flexibility.

If no red flags have come up by this point, after asking about pay and availability you should ask the rest of the phone-interview questions. You should have studied the resume and written specific questions pertaining to it. Include questions about whether the applicant has worked in similar environments, and whether he enjoyed them. For example, you might ask about working in a small office. Some people really thrive in an office with a bigger staff, and some like small offices.

Make the phone interview short if you find out something you don't like. Make it longer and ask as many questions as you can if you like the person and she meets your requirements. Please note that you should ask open-ended questions, not leading questions. For example, instead of asking, "Are you available from 9:00 to 4:00 Monday through Friday," you should say, "Tell me about your availability. What hours will work for you?" and "What are your ideal hours?" Use this same technique for the in-person interview.

You will be amazed by the things you'll find out in phone interviews if you follow these guidelines. Once, an applicant slipped up and told me her goal was to move out of the county in six months to pursue a completely different career. You can be sure I ended the interview moments later, without letting on why.

If you are sure you like the candidate enough to do a live interview, make an appointment for the interview before you hang up. If you are unsure or if you don't like the candidate, you can say, "Thank you so much for your time. Right now I'm still in the process of collecting resumes. If I want to request an interview, I'll call you by next Friday." That way, the person knows that if you don't call by Friday, he hasn't been selected.

Nowadays, you aren't expected to let candidates know whether they are rejected unless they get to the final interview stage. So if you decide not to do a live interview with the person you spoke to on the phone, you do not need to contact her.

Create, Send, and Screen the Email Interview Questions and Responses

If you have a rather technical position or one that requires lots of writing, or if you want to screen the person in any other way, you may wish to create an email with a series of questions for the applicant to answer in writing. You may ask him to describe exactly what kinds of jobs he has done on a CAD program, for example, or what kinds of correspondence he has done in prior jobs. If you have a job that requires a certain value system, you can ask the applicant how his personal values fit with the company's mission. If it's a sales position that requires email correspondence with clients, you can ask the applicant to provide detail about the sales jobs he has held and his sales rank compared to the other sales staff.

I recently screened resumes for a client and found one with a well-written cover letter and a well-written resume. I knew that the open position required a good deal of correspondence via email and Word documents, so I sent an email asking what the applicant was looking for in a job. The applicant's email response was full of grammatical errors, and the language was awkward. Clearly, someone else had written the person's cover letter and resume. Needless to say, the applicant wasn't invited for an interview. In certain instances, you may wish to do the email screening before the telephone interview.

Email the List of Jobs Form

Once you have screened the applicant by email and phone, ask her to fill out the List of Jobs Form and bring it to the interview. Often, some or much of the information listed on the form is missing from the person's resume. Study the form for inconsistencies and make notes for questions. For example, if there is a timeframe where no jobs are listed, you'll want to know why. During the in-person interview, you'll also want to ask why the applicant left each job on the form.

If the form is filled out properly, it will give you all the information you'll need for the job interview, as well as what you'll need for checking references. Make sure you get this form back right away, before you do the interview.

Never forget, you are looking for an A+ employee.

Hold the In-Person Interviews and Administer the Skills Tests

This is it! You've done your homework, and now it's time to do the hardest part—the interview. Take note: This is where employers tend to make the biggest mistakes. This is your chance to get the applicant to talk for long enough that you get all the information you want. Zip your lip and let the candidate talk!

Don't spend time trying to shield the applicant from uncomfortable questions. I don't advocate making people uncomfortable, like some tough job interviewers do, but I think most interviewers do the opposite—they spend time tipping off the applicant to the answers they want to hear, instead of drawing out the truth. Do you see the difference? You're there to let the applicant reveal herself to you, and you can only do this by asking non-leading, open-ended questions, and by keep-ing quiet yourself for most of the time.

When you ask an open-ended question and the applicant gives a short answer of a couple of sentences, don't rescue him by asking the next question. Instead, just smile encouragingly, nod, and keep your mouth closed. He will keep talking to fill the space, knowing by your expression that you want to hear more. This will keep the applicant talk-ing past the answers he has already rehearsed, and this is when the truth really comes out.

If you sense the applicant's discomfort that comes at this stage, don't rescue him—let him fumble for the right words. The things people will give away about themselves when you do this may surprise you. If you get a too-short answer and the applicant doesn't take the hint that you want to hear more, just ask, "What else?" or say, "Tell me more."

Also, don't spend time telling the applicant all about your company until *after* you love him. Only when you get to that point do you start to sell your company to him.

Interview Tips

Refer to this list of interview tips before you start interviewing:

1. Print out your interview questions on paper, with lots of space between each question for notes. Also, have a separate paper with a list of your qualities printed down the left-hand side. Make notes next to each quality as you interview the candidate.

2. Take copious notes! You won't accurately remember who said what unless you do this. Use the sheet with the list of qualities and skills, as well as the sheet with your interview questions.

3. Ask open-ended questions and statements, such as "Tell me about yourself," "What did you like about your last job?" "Dislike?" and "What are you looking for in a job?" If you're trying to find out whether the applicant is organized, don't ask her that outright. Instead, ask her how she keeps herself organized in various parts of her life. If she says that all of her CDs and DVDs are arranged in strict alphabetical order and

she uses different colors for different items on her calendar, you can probably infer that she is organized.

4. Zip your lip! Nod your head, smile, and listen. Ask open-ended questions that invite very long answers. If the applicant still gives short answers, say politely, "Okay, thank you. What else can you tell me about that?"

5. Be curious. Really listen and make sure you connect the dots about everything you can think of, and ask for clarification where needed. For example, if an applicant has done some consulting on the side but has mostly been in the workplace, ask why she hasn't gone into consulting full-time. She might say that she wants to but she hasn't landed a big client yet. This should send up a red flag. By the end of the interview, you should understand what motivates your applicant and why she has made the decisions she has. Understanding what's important to your applicant is the only way you'll be able to find someone who will be happy for a long time. Until you really have this understanding about your applicant, keep the interview going.

6. Be gracious without trying to rescue the applicant. There is no use in grilling the applicant or making her more uncomfortable than she already is. On the other hand, it's your job to ask difficult questions so you can get to the truth—it's not your job to shield the applicant.

7. During the interview, use the List of Jobs Form to give yourself a chronological history of the applicant's jobs and the reason why she left each job. Take notes. If you see a gap in employment, ask why she left the workplace. People sometimes say amazing things, such as, "I spent two years in rehab." (Of course, they usually will try to cover up these things.)

8. Take lots of time if you like the applicant. You will be spending huge amounts of time with this person, and you're crazy if you aren't willing to spend as long as it takes to find out everything you want to know about her. Your interview could and should take hours—unless a red flag comes up.

9. Stop the interview as soon as a red flag comes up. Don't waste your time or the applicant's by extending the meeting. Gracefully let her finish her answer and then say something such as, "I really appreciate you coming down for this first interview. I will be interviewing quite a few more people. If you're selected for a second interview, I'll let you know by this Friday." As I mentioned earlier, you aren't expected to tell people that they weren't selected at this stage of the game.

10. If you really like the applicant, show her the daily checklist and explain that she will be filling it out each day. Carefully watch her response. Does she glance at it and say, "Sure, that's fine"? Or does she really look at it and say, "Great, I love checklists"? Also, give the applicant an evaluation form if you have one. This lets her know what you're looking for.

11. Make sure you ask the applicant how much she made at each of her previous jobs. The wage or salary will likely be inflated, so be sure you ask the references what she was making. You will need this information later, when you're negotiating pay.

12. Remember, by the end of the interview you should understand what motivates the applicant and whether she will fit in the job at your company. Understanding what's important to the applicant is the only way you'll be able to find someone who will be happy for a long time.

13. If you love the applicant, and you have filled in all of the blanks next to the list of qualities and skills, and no red flags have come up, do the following before she leaves:

    a. Ask her to sign a form giving you permission to do a background check. You can get this form from your local background-check company or search the Internet for one.

    b. Give her a standard job application form that you can buy from an office-supply store or find on the Internet. By the way, in general, if you get forms on the Internet, make sure they're made for use in your state. Some states are stricter than others.

c. Review the list of jobs form with the applicant and make sure all the contact information is there. Notice that this form asks for the names and current phone numbers of direct supervisors (not human resources). If the supervisor has left the company, ask the applicant to track her down and get a current number so you can talk to her. A word of caution: In this day and age of cell phones, you need to be aware that the person you are talking to could just be a friend of the applicant posing as a former supervisor.

d. Make sure you have "sold" the job by telling the applicant what's great about your company and workplace.

Even if you have done your homework well before the in-person interview, you will fairly often find things you didn't expect. Recently, I interviewed an applicant for a client. The applicant carefully asked me who her supervisor would be and how much oversight there would be. She declined the position when she learned that there would be lots of accountability via checklists and that she would have to follow the systems in place before suggesting improvements to her supervisor. Fortunately, the applicant was honest enough to realize she wasn't a good fit for the position.

Interview Questions for Job Applicants

Following are some open-ended questions and comments you might pose during the interview:

- What did you like about your last job? (Ask this about all of the jobs on the applicant's resume.)
- What was your boss like at this job? How did he or she get the best out of you?
- What did you like least about the job? Why did you leave?
- What will your boss say when you go in to resign from your current job?
- How many levels of management did you interact with? What was your communication about?

- Who was your favorite manager and why? Who was your least favorite and why?
- Describe your favorite work environments. How about your least favorite?
- What are your short-, medium-, and long-term goals?
- What do you think you are best at? Worst at?
- Why did you apply for this job?
- What do you know about the company?
- What do you expect out of this job?
- What are your reservations about working here?
- Tell me about yourself. What else can you tell me about yourself?
- What are your goals?
- How would you define a good work atmosphere?
- What kinds of co-workers do you like? Dislike?
- Can you get me copies of your evaluations?

Following are some specific but non-leading questions you can ask during the interview:

- How much do you need to earn at this job?
- What was your starting and ending wage or salary at your previous job?
- What are some examples of how you stay organized at home and work?
- What other day-to-day job activities did you have that we haven't discussed?
- How do you rank among your peers? (This is especially important for sales positions.)
- What kind of person do you best get along with? Worst?
- What do you do when your workload gets too heavy? Too slow?

- Describe the best manager you ever had. How did he give you direction and feedback?

A note about questions: Be sure to cover the above questions, but also realize that you will be asking additional questions based on what you observe and what you decide you need to know about the person based on those observations. Remember, you're like a detective, trying to figure out whether the applicant is going to love this job. Try to figure out whether there are things that won't make this a good match. Often applicants aren't very good judges about whether they will be a good fit for a job.

The rest of the questions below represent the types of questions many people study for in advance. I'm not necessarily recommending that you use these—only that you understand what questions people might be practicing for.

Basic questions

- Tell me about yourself.
- What do you know about our company?
- Why should we hire you?
- What can you do for us that someone else can't?
- What do you look for in a job?
- What skills and qualifications are essential for success in the position of _____?
- How long would it take for you to make a meaningful contribution?
- How does this assignment fit into your overall career plan?
- Describe your management style.
- What do you believe is the most difficult part of supervising people?
- Why are you looking for a new career?
- How would your colleagues describe you?
- How would your boss describe you?

- How would you describe yourself?
- What do you think of your present or past boss?
- What were the five most significant accomplishments in your last assignment?
- What have been the five most significant accomplishments in your career so far?
- Can you work well under deadlines or pressure?
- How much do you expect to earn if we offer you this position?
- What other positions are you considering?
- Have you kept up in your field with additional training?
- What are your career goals?
- What are your strong points?
- What are your weak points?
- How did you do in school?
- What position do you expect to have in two to five years?
- If you took the job, what would you accomplish in the first year?
- What kind of hours are you used to working or would you like to work?
- Do you have your reference list with you?
- Can you explain your salary history?
- What questions didn't I ask that you expected?
- Do you have any questions for me?

Situational questions
- Give an example of how you got a vendor/customer/employee to cooperate.
- Give an example of a time when you made a mistake and what you did to make sure it didn't happen again.
- Have you ever had to make unpopular decisions? Tell me about them.

- Describe a situation in which you were able to use persuasion to successfully convince someone to see things your way.
- Describe an instance when you had to think on your feet to extricate yourself from a difficult situation.
- Give me a specific example of a time when you used good judgment and logic to solve a problem.
- Describe a time when you were faced with problems or stresses that tested your coping skills.
- Give an example of a time when you had to be relatively quick in coming to a decision.
- Describe a time when you had to use your written communication skills to get an important point across.
- Give me a specific occasion when you conformed to a policy with which you didn't agree.
- Give me an example of an important goal you set in the past and tell me about your success in reaching it.
- Tell me about a time when you had to go above and beyond the call of duty to get a job done.
- Give me an example of a time when you were able to successfully communicate with another person, even when that individual may not have liked you personally (or vice versa).
- Sometimes it's easy to get in over your head. Describe a situation in which you had to request assistance on a project or an assignment.
- Tell me about a time when you worked with a colleague who wasn't completing her share of the work. Who, if anyone, did you talk to about it? Did the manager take any steps to correct your colleague? Did you agree or disagree with the manager's actions?
- Describe a situation in which you had to arrive at a compromise or guide others to a compromise.
- What steps do you follow to study a problem before making a decision?

- We can sometimes identify a small problem and fix it before it becomes a major problem. Give an examples of how you have done this.

- In a supervisory or group-leader role, have you ever had to discipline or counsel an employee or group member? What was the nature of the discipline? What steps did you take? How did that make you feel? How did you prepare yourself?

- Recall a time from your work experience when your manager or supervisor was unavailable and a problem arose. What was the nature of the problem? How did you handle the situation? How did it make you feel?

- Recall a time when you were assigned what you considered to be a complex project. Specifically, what steps did you take to prepare for and finish the project? Were you happy with the outcome? What one step would you have done differently if given the chance?

- Tell me about some situations in which you've had to adjust quickly to changes over which you had no control. What was the impact of the changes on you?

- Describe some times when you weren't very satisfied with your performance. What did you do about it?

- Give me an example from your current job that demonstrates your persistence.

Hold the Second Interview and Skills Test

If you love the applicant, arrange for her to come back soon for a second interview, which will include a skills test. To put the applicant at ease, you can call it a skills demo. Don't wait too long; if you have a great applicant, you should have her back in just a couple of days. I've seen an excellent candidate snapped up by the competition many a time—even when the job market was extremely soft.

Check References

Checking references is often the Achilles' heel of job searches. For some reason, everyone has heard about employers being sued for giving negative feedback about an employee. In fact, this is *extremely rare*. As I mention in the legal section of this book, you're much more likely to be sued for other things than for giving negative feedback. But, because employers fear they cannot get the information, they give up or don't try very hard. This is not a good idea! You can finesse this stage of the process and get the information you need.

First, avoid HR departments, because they are strict about only giving you the dates the employee worked. Often owners and supervisors are willing to go much further. If you reach an owner and she seems reluctant to talk much, let her know you understand her position and that anything she tells you will be confidential. (By all means, keep all of your reference information confidential.) This will protect all parties from a lawsuit. Talk to her owner-to-owner. Do the best you can to get her talking.

Once you get someone talking, you can often get a lot of information. One technique that can work very well is to start with the easy questions you know the person will answer. Then slowly work your way to the more specific questions. If the person hesitates, let her know you understand her position and that you will be discreet.

Do beware; some owners will give their former employee a good reference just to do the person a misguided favor. But one question most people will answer is, "Would you hire this person again?" If she says no, there's no use in trying to get more information about the applicant. If she says yes, it logically follows that she should be willing to talk about the applicant's good qualities.

Once you have the former employer going on the good qualities, start asking very specific questions, such as, "Is he organized? Is he super accurate? Is he conscientious? Is he good at math?" Often you can get the former employer to tip you off about the candidate's weaknesses. Sometimes you learn a lot by listening carefully to the person's tone of voice.

Here is a list of things to remember:

1. Call the correct person. Avoid HR; talk to the direct supervisor and one supervisor above the direct supervisor if you can.

2. Call *all* the references—use the list of jobs form you got from the applicant.

3. Ask why the person left the job and see whether that reason is the same one the applicant gave for leaving the job.

4. Don't give up if you get some resistance. Stick with it and finesse the situation to get the information you're looking for.

5. Ask the former employer whether she would rehire the applicant if she could.

6. Use your list of qualities and skills and make sure you ask about all of them!

7. Take good notes.

Here is a short true story about reference checks.

Reference Checks

A client who is an architect ran an ad for office help. Attached to a resume were two glowing letters of recommendation on letterhead. The owner cut corners and didn't call the supervisors who signed the letters. He didn't especially like the applicant's personality, but he was in a rush to get help and wanted to hire someone from the first batch of applicants. He did, however, have a daily checklist prepared in advance.

The employee's performance was poor from day one. She never completed all of the items on her daily checklist. Tasks were left undone. Then the owner discovered the employee was suing a former employer, and she used office time to work on her case! The owner caught her taking company letterhead and writing letters of recommendation that were supposed to be from him to support her court case. He then called the former employers whose letterheads were used for the employee's original letters of recommendation. Both owners denied writing the letters and told him the woman was a terrible employee.

The owner fired the employee, who then filed for unemployment. The owner went to the local state court that handles this type of case to contest the unemployment. (If an employee is fired, she usually isn't granted unemployment, although it fully depends on the judge's ruling). By then, the ex-employee was showing signs of mental illness. She threatened the owner with letters and phone calls. Her behavior in court was so odd that the judge ruled against her.

So, by failing to check references, the owner suffered many negative consequences: His office work didn't get done properly, he was harassed and threatened, and he had to pay a labor-law attorney to go to court. Talk about stress!

Never forget, you are looking for an A+ employee.

Do Background Checks and Online Checks

If you've gone this far and you still have an outstanding applicant, it's time to do a background check. Why is this a good idea? First, you don't want an employee who is under too much financial stress. It may affect his job performance, and it may be too tempting for him to steal. So, pay to have someone do a financial background check. They aren't expensive.

My understanding is that there are some legal guidelines about which job positions you should limit yourself to as far as background checks. Any employee with access to funds or who handles customer funds or credit cards is a green light. I also suggest doing a background check on anyone who has access to valuable inventory or other access to theft. If in doubt, you can double-check with your labor-law attorney on this.

If the applicant is rejected due to the background check, you are legally obligated to tell him. As I mentioned earlier, there are any number of reasons you may decide against a person, and sometimes it's best just to tell him you found someone more qualified. I'm not giving legal advice here…

You are also on legal thin ice if you reject someone for the information you got by going online and checking him out. So if you do this, it's probably best not to mention it to the applicant. But it's a free country, and here are some things you can do online:

1. criminalsearches.com is a database of all kinds of criminal arrests and convictions, from murders to traffic tickets, drawn directly from courthouse records. You will need the information on the job application for this search. It's quick and easy.
2. Do a Google search on the applicant.
3. Do a Facebook search on the applicant.

Here is a quick story about a client who was a plumber. He hired an administrative assistant/bookkeeper. Shortly thereafter, he started dating someone who worked at the county offices. She looked up the employee's name in the database and found out she had been convicted of embezzlement twice! Needless to say, the plumber let the employee go right away.

This is a good time mention that it helps to have a sense of humor when you're screening resumes. I have seen photos and postings on Facebook and Google+ that make it easy to screen out the applicant. You really wonder what they were thinking!

Make a Hiring Decision

First of all, if you are unsure about a person, don't hire her. Follow the maxim, "When in doubt, don't." Never forget, you are looking for an A+ employee. You should be very enthusiastic about the person. Don't hire the applicant just because she is the best of the bunch. If you don't love someone from this batch of applicants, start over and interview the next batch. You'll be so glad you did!

And remember, you need to really love the person's personality. One of my clients was looking to fill a specialized marketing position as his toy company expanded. He found two good applicants and was having a hard time deciding between them. One person had skills that were more specialized for his industry, but he didn't love her personality. However, he hired her anyway. The new employee soon started rubbing her supervisor the wrong way. They let her stay for over a year, and each day this person caused more drama and discomfort in the workplace. When they finally parted ways, it was a giant relief for the rest of the staff.

Make sure you have a solid understanding of the applicant's levels of all the qualities and skills you have on your list, and that you love her personality.

Say Yes or No to the Applicant

Finally, the time has come to say yes or no to the applicant. But how?

How to Say Yes

When you inform your applicant that he has been chosen, you should have a firm idea of how much the starting pay will be. This should be based on the applicant's prior pay and on where his experience fits in the pay range you're offering. If your pay range is $15 to $17 per hour depending on experience, and the applicant has been earning $16 per hour, you might want to offer $15 per hour as starting pay, with the chance for him to work his way to the upper ranges. You need to communicate what the starting pay will be and prepare for some negotiating if the applicant asks for more.

By this time you should have agreed upon the initial hours to be worked, while keeping in mind the broader agreement if the position requires flexibility.

The main point is to set a date and get your employee working as soon as possible. If you delay, anything can happen and you might lose your applicant. Act quickly! I have often heard business owners say they didn't get back to their star applicant quickly, and someone else hired him—even during a period with very high unemployment.

How to Say No

If the applicant knows she is one of the finalists, you have gone through all or most of the previous steps, and you decide to either go with someone else or pass up this person, here's what you can say: "Thank you so much for your time. As you know, we were very interested in hiring you, but I'm so sorry—we have found someone more qualified." You might turn around and post the ad again the next day, but it's still a good policy to be vague about why you rejected the applicant.

Chapter 3:

Legal Issues

This book isn't intended to give you legal advice. However, it was written with the law in mind. My advice to all of my clients is to have a good labor-law attorney. A good attorney should be available for simple questions by email or phone. If you're concise, you can send him an email, and he will send you a succinct response. The hourly rate is a normal attorney's rate, but the bill can be very low if it takes him only a few minutes to respond. Spending $50 or $100 here or there on questions can save you thousands of dollars later.

Over the years, I have noticed that the two main issues employers are sued for are labor laws and discrimination. In general, the labor-law lawsuits usually have merit, because employers tend to be sloppy about enforcing things such as breaks, lunch, and overtime. On the other hand, in my experience discrimination lawsuits are usually based on unfounded accusations. Somehow, many workers have found out that they can find an unsavory attorney, make a false claim, and basically blackmail an employer into settling for an amount that costs less than going to court. There's not much you can do about discrimination lawsuits (except carry insurance to cover it), but there is a lot you can do about labor-law lawsuits.

It's a good idea to be aware of the discrimination issue while you're hiring so you can avoid the pitfalls. You can protect yourself in three main ways.

1. If the applicant doesn't know why you've rejected him, it will be hard for him to make a claim against you. Therefore, don't give him that information. When you tell him why he didn't get the job, use a stock answer: "I found someone more qualified." Or, if it was someone you interviewed twice, say, "We really liked you, and you were one of our top candidates, but we found someone more qualified."

2. Avoid asking potential hires directly about themselves. Instead of saying, "How old are you? Do you have kids?" you can say, "Tell me about yourself." This way, you can't be accused of discriminating against the applicant for having kids or being too old. Just keep nodding your head, listening, and asking the applicant to tell you more until he has covered everything you were wondering about. Remember, you aren't allowed to discriminate about anything—age, sex, weight, religion, race, kids, illness, disability, alcoholism, and so on. So don't react negatively to anything you hear, or you could find yourself the target of a lawsuit.

3. Don't tell the applicant if any of his references said anything negative about him. This could potentially make the former employer the subject of a lawsuit, but it's extremely rare. My personal approach to giving references to potential bosses of my former employees is this: If I loved the employee and can wholeheartedly recommend her, I am very open and candid. If I wouldn't rehire the employee, I state that right away and don't give any details about why. I'm not an expert on the finer legal details, but I believe it's the specific details that, when repeated to the applicant, can create a potential lawsuit.

Now that you've hired your new employee, how do you make sure he thrives in your workplace? That is the subject of Part Two of this book.

Part Two

How to Make Sure Your New Employee Succeeds: Tools and Skills

All companies have cultures and operating styles that come directly from the top. If you're having trouble in any area, look in the mirror and figure out why. There is a saying that "every problem is a management problem." If you have employee problems, it is because you hired poorly, you trained poorly, or you failed to let an employee go as quickly as you should have. Or, you have a management style that is rubbing your employees the wrong way.

Your sacred duty with your employees is to do the following: Make your expectations clear, invest in training, give your employees the resources they need to do their jobs well, manage each employee according to her personality style, give clear and timely feedback, treat your employees with unfailing respect and politeness, be a good role model, hold your employees accountable for the results you want, and make sure they never fear their paycheck will bounce or be late.

I have often told my clients that managing employees is very similar to being a good parent. After all, adults are just grown-up kids, and human nature pretty much stays the same. People of all ages need clear, consistent, respectful direction. They need to be allowed creativity within the guidelines set by the boss or parent. They need to be listened to, respected, and responded to with a clear yes or no. For the most part, they respond better to positive discipline or incentives than to punishment; in fact, punishment rarely works for adults.

What *does* work is respectfully discussing how things can be improved and turning every mistake into a learning experience. As with all management, modeling in this case is important. If you inform an employee that you made a mistake in how you managed her and then you show her you can correct the mistake and manage that specific thing well in the future, you can be an inspiration to her.

So, just how do you do all of these things? You use a combination of tools and skills. I will review the tools you need and the skills you need to develop to use the tools properly, because an improperly used tool won't work. Many employers have told me, "I've tried checklists—they don't work," or "I've tried incentives—they don't work." All of the tools I give you can work beautifully if you're willing to learn how to use them well.

If you expect your employees to learn and master new skills, you will need to be a good role model and show them that you are a good boss. If you make a mistake, apologize for it and explain what you plan to do differently in the future. How long it will take you to turn your workplace into a healthy one will depend on how quickly you are willing to make the necessary changes. Some of my clients take years to make the transition, and it's still worth it. However, I recently had a client transform his retail store from a headache to a smoothly running operation in just a few months by fully embracing the tools and changing his management style so that they work. He now has the confidence to work much less because he knows his employees are doing a good job. In addition, he has freed up his own time so that he can work with me on profitability issues. We have already put an extra $30,000 a year on his bottom line, and we have laid out the steps to add another $50,000 to $60,000.

Chapter 4

The Tools for the Job

Following is a list of tools you can use to manage most effectively. The better you manage, the longer your employees will stay, and the more opportunity you will have to increase profits.

1. Organizational chart
2. Job descriptions
3. Daily and procedural checklists
4. Training
5. Promotion path
6. Evaluations
7. Pay policies
8. Reports
9. Incentives
10. General-management techniques

I will discuss each of these tools and the skills you need to make them work. If you've hired the right employees, and if you learn to use these tools and master the skills needed, you can run a happy, healthy organization.

The Organizational Chart

It might surprise you to find out that organizational charts, or *org charts*, are just as important for a small company as for a corporation. An org chart helps business owners create a chain of command and delineate job roles so that you don't have overlapping responsibilities or gaps. You should have only one person responsible for each job position so that accountability is clear.

An org chart also helps you, as a small-business owner, see how many job positions you are responsible for. This helps you acknowledge that fact and work with it rather than against it. Once you have seen how many roles you have taken on, it is highly advisable that you assign certain regular times each week to take on that role and put all of your attention to it. Clear your mind, for example, of marketing while you are tackling financial issues. Don't try to carry all of your concerns around in a big cloud above your head. Pigeonhole them as much as you can, and you can feel secure that on Tuesday afternoon, for example, you will sit down and make your marketing decisions, so you don't have to worry about them on the other days. (One of the hottest issues my clients and I work on is time management. Once I give them time-management tools plus direction on how to use them, their stress level generally goes way down.)

Each position on the org chart has a title and a job description. You can add names later, but you start with the title. As a small-business owner, you may have several different job titles—for example, president, CFO, and marketing manager. You may have an operations manager who is responsible for managing your employees in operations. You may stand in as a crew foreman who is technically managed by the operations manager, one of your own employees. It can get complicated, so it's important for all staff to understand the chain of command. This is especially important in husband-and-wife teams, so you don't drive your employees crazy by having two different people managing them.

Take a look at the following chart and count how many of these positions you hold in your own company. If your company has five employees or fewer, you probably hold the uppermost eight or so positions in

```
                    ┌─────────────────┐
                    │ Board of Directors │
                    │   or Owner      │
                    └─────────────────┘
                            │
                    ┌─────────────────┐
                    │      CEO        │
                    │  or President   │
                    └─────────────────┘
              ┌─────────────┴──────────────────┐
       ┌──────────────┐              ┌──────────────────┐
       │    CFO       │              │ General Manager  │
       │  Controller  │              └──────────────────┘
       └──────────────┘
    ┌──────────┬──────────┐      ┌──────────┬──────────┬──────────┐
┌──────────┐┌──────────┐┌──────────┐      ┌──────────┐┌──────────┐
│Accounting││Finance & ││Operations│      │Sales & Mktg││   HR     │
│Supervisor││Purchasing││ Manager  │      │ Manager  ││ Manager  │
│          ││Assistant ││          │      └──────────┘└──────────┘
└──────────┘└──────────┘└──────────┘
┌──────────┐      ┌──────────┐┌──────────┐┌──────────┐┌──────────┐
│Bookkeeper│      │Installation││Plant Maint &││Sales & Cust Svc││Advertising and│
│          │      │Crew Leader││Repair Tech││  Rep     ││Promo Assistant│
└──────────┘      └──────────┘└──────────┘└──────────┘└──────────┘
                  ┌──────────┐
                  │Installation│
                  │  Techs   │
                  └──────────┘
```

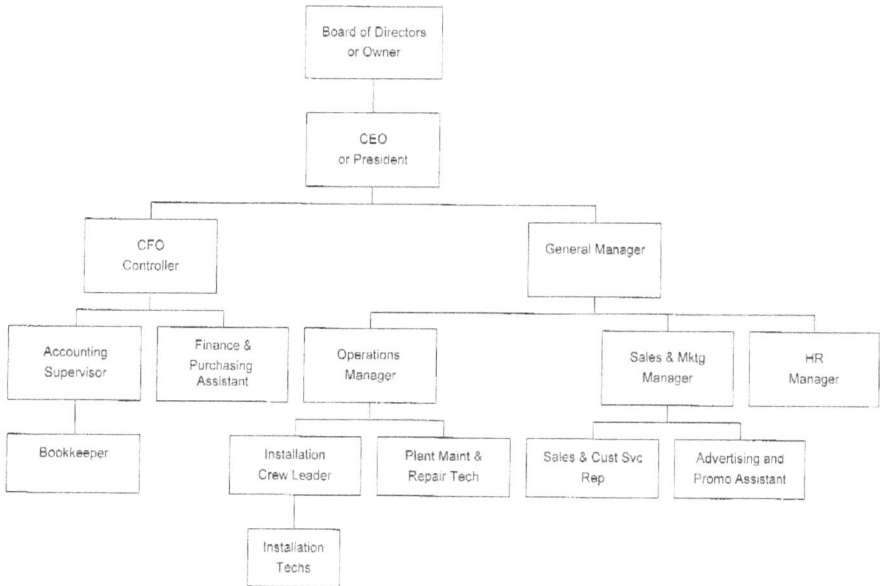

this chart. If you have 10 employees, you probably still hold five or six of these titles. If you have more than 20 employees, you may be able to afford a full-time general manager, which greatly reduces the number of positions you must hold. Meanwhile, you must act as general manager yourself.

You can see how important it is to delegate effectively when you're wearing so many hats. You have to do each job only part-time, which means you must have a very strong team to keep daily operations humming smoothly and efficiently. You may work for only a few hours a week as the marketing manager or the CFO, for example, so you must have competent people who can do 95 percent of the work for you. Only if you leverage yourself effectively, by delegating, can each department possibly work smoothly. If you are a very small company with one to five employees, you will be able to delegate much less; therefore, you must work within the hours you have and spend an appropriate amount of time each week in each department.

The organizational chart gives you a good perspective from which to understand a healthy chain of command. Do not undermine your managers by going directly to their employees if you see something wrong; instead, tell the manager what's wrong and have him address it with the employee in question. Similarly, don't let your employees bypass their manager and go directly to you with problems. If the employee can't work out the problem with the supervisor, she should ask for a meeting with all three of you to sort out the problem. In the meeting, don't undermine or criticize the manager. If he is mishandling the situation, meet with him separately to get him back on track. And don't discipline or correct employees in front of other employees unless you have to—it's humiliating to the employee.

The chain of command, as illustrated in the org chart, is all about delegation. Each manager delegates as much responsibility as possible to her team. The manager should encourage employees to think for themselves to help them develop their judgment. A good manager doesn't let an employee bring problems to her and leave them in her lap. When an employee comes to you with a problem or a decision that needs to be made, you should first ask him what he thinks the solution is. If you don't agree, ask him to try again. Once you have determined what action to take, put it back into the employee's lap and have him finish the task. Otherwise, you'll encourage your staff to dump anything they don't want to deal with in your lap. Many business owners develop this dependency habit with their staff. If you have middle managers or supervisors of any type, don't just skim over these last two paragraphs—really study them and make sure you follow all of these rules.

One other point about the org chart: Use it as a tool to decide on the next person you should hire. Generally, the lower the position on the chart, the lower the wage. You generally want to delegate the lowest-wage positions first to help maximize profits. For example, instead of hiring a sales manager who spends much of her time taking customer-service calls, consider hiring a really good customer-service person at a lower wage—that person can take on some assistant-manager or team-leader duties while you hold the sales manager title.

I just met with a vibrant, fast-growing company founded by two women who met in college. They are so much in sync about all of the activities and decisions that they have made to expand the company that they never bothered to delegate specfic responsibilities to each of themselves. The result is that they spend too much time wondering whether the other person has just done the very task they were about to do. It was a big relief, as well as a timesaver, to create an org chart to streamline and delineate responsibilities, accountability, and tasks. They were freed up to each do her own part to move the company forward.

Job Descriptions as a Management Tool

Once you've created your org chart, you will have titles for each position. For each title, now you can make a job description.

You already developed your job description before hiring your employee. (Please refer to the Hiring section.) However, if you have an existing employee who doesn't have a job description, it will be helpful to develop one with the employee's input. This makes the pay range clear, among other things. That way, when you get to evaluation time, the parameters for pay raises will be clear. Not having this in place can cause ill will in a number of ways.

Another good reason for creating job descriptions for existing (or new) employees is that job descriptions delineate general responsibilities. This helps tremendously with accountability. For example, an employee may not have been instructed to empty the trash, but the job description holds that person accountable for keeping the workplace neat, clean, and organized. If the supervisor points out a smelly, overflowing wastebasket, the excuse that "no one told me to empty it" won't fly because of the job description.

Daily and Procedural Checklists

First, a word about checklists, repeated from the first part of the book. Often my clients feel uncomfortable giving their employees checklists because they think it may be demeaning and it's treating the employee like a child. On the contrary, it gives the employee direction, structure, and a feeling of accomplishment at the end of the day when everything is checked off. Many things aren't covered by the checklists and will require the employee's judgment and creativity. But if the employees aren't instructed on how you want the everyday basics done, they will spend their time reinventing the wheel and doing things differently from how you want them. Checklists are a basic of quality management, as explained in this excellent article.

Remember, there are two kinds of checklists: the daily checklist and the procedural checklist. Employees will use their daily checklists every day. Any items on the daily checklist that need more specific instructions are detailed on the procedural checklists.

Checklists can really work or they can be ineffective and ignored by your employees. So, how do you make checklists really work for you? Follow the 11-point checklist in the "Skills" section below to make sure yours are successful.

Many of my clients have told me that as soon as they implemented their checklists, they felt as though a huge burden and workload were lifted. This is because in the past, when the employees left for the day, the owner was left to do everything that was unfinished. After the checklists were implemented—voilà, almost every thing was actually done at the end of the day. And if things weren't done, it was easy to pinpoint what wasn't done and who was responsible. If an item is on the checklist, the employee can be alerted. If an item isn't on the checklist, it can be added.

Recently, I met with a client who owns a pizza restaurant. She was so upset by all of the details that weren't getting done that she was close to tears. After two meetings we had two checklists in place, and the owner's body language had radically changed. Within a couple of weeks, all of the checklists were in place, and she was so relieved that she looked as if she'd had a facelift!

Health care's long to-do list

By Darshak Sanghavi
SPECIAL TO THE CHRONICLE

Modern doctors are arguably the most hyper-educated professionals in the world, requiring eight years of higher education, followed by three to 10 years of residency and subspecialty training.

And yet, according to well-respected studies from the Rand Corp., roughly half the time doctors fail to provide the right preventive and acute medical care for adults and children for everything from ear infections to heart attacks to sexually transmitted diseases. Doctors long ago discovered treatments for the conditions. Why, then, do they so often fail to apply them correctly?

The Checklist Manifesto
How to Get Things Right
By Atul Gawande
(Metropolitan Books; 209 pages; $24.50)

In his compelling book, "The Checklist Manifesto: How to Get Things Right," the surgeon and writer Atul Gawande expands on the ideas popularized in his 2007 New Yorker essay about the remarkable impact of simple checklists on medical care. Fundamentally, he notes, there are two reasons for failure: ignorance (not yet knowing how to do something) and ineptitude (failing to apply what is already known). The former can be forgiven, but the latter rightly arouses anger and judgment.

The most intriguing chapters are those in which Gawande hangs out with sk scra er builders, sous chefs and airline safety officers to understand why other professions have far outpaced medicine in breaking down complex processes to deliver reliable results.

Centuries ago, he writes, builders used to be a lot like today's doctors, where a "Master Builder" was given total autonomy to construct projects like Notre Dame and the U.S. Capitol building. But making skyscrapers became so mind-bogglingly complex that no one builder could handle it. So builders created elaborate production checklists (they "ensure that the knowledge of hundreds, perhaps thousands, is put to use in the right place at the right time in the right way") and, more important, specified key communication tasks between experts like elevator installers and engineers. Today, less than 0.00002 percent of buildings fail though they're more complex than ever.

But in medicine, Gawande notes that "a lone Master Physician with a prescription pad" still works in a system that is "completely uncoordinated." To explain how good checklists are created, Gawande turns to engineers and aviation airline pilots, more than any other field, have pioneered the science of checklists.

Following the spectacular crash of Boeing's "flying fortress" test bomber in 1935, Boeing engineers created an index-card-size checklist of critical tasks that was so effective, not a single of the 13,000 planes ever crashed again. Most recently, Capt. Chesley Sullenberger's 2009 "miracle of the Hudson" landing is owed to an emergency checklist.

These checklists, argues Gawande, should be widely used in health care. The successful ones accomplish two things. First, they ensure that narrowly specific "stupid stuff" isn't missed, like allergies or proper antibiotics. Just as important, the checklists also build in communication checks to ensure people work as a team.

In 2008, for example, he and a team of researchers from the World Health Organization deployed a 19-point pre-surgery checklist to be used in hospitals worldwide from Tanzania to Toronto; incredibly, major complications dropped by a third and death rates were cut in half.

Gawande spins out the implications of his project: Couldn't checklists be expanded to address heart attacks, strokes, kidney failure or seizures, whose treatment is surely not more complicated than flying a massive bomber?

For too long, medicine has been insulated from the kinds of quality and process improvement that's become standard in all kinds of industries. In calling attention to the power of checklists, Gawande argues convincingly and eloquently for doctors to learn from others. After all, our lives may depend on it.

Darshak Sanghavi is Slate's health care columnist and a contributing editor for Parents. E-mail him at books@sfchronicle.com

How to Create a Daily Checklist

Sit down with your employees and create a chronological list of everything they do during the day. Exactly what do they need to do when they first arrive? What time do they go get the mail? When do shipments have to be ready for UPS? And so on... Add once-a-week items to the daily list and mention the day of the week they should be done. Do the same with monthly, quarterly, and yearly items. For any items that need separate written procedures, create a procedural checklist. Always refer to each procedural checklist on the daily checklist, or else they will get forgotten. Even if you don't have your accounts-payable procedural checklist created yet, refer to it on the daily checklist as though it does exist, and that will remind you to make it.

How to Create a Procedural Checklist

Let's say you're ready to create your payroll checklist. Sit down with your bookkeeper and write down every step she takes. Include which software menu items to choose and any other mouse clicks, passwords, and so on that someone new would need to know if she had to step in. Write these quickly by hand or type them on a laptop while you watch. Then go back later and rewrite the list in the format below. Have your bookkeeper use it and make suggestions for corrections. Be alert for anything that you think needs improving as you write up the checklist the first time.

As I mentioned, every procedural checklist should be referred to on your daily checklist, or else it will be forgotten. In this example, you will have a daily checklist item that says something like, "On the 3rd and the 16th of the month, print out the payroll checklist and begin payroll."

Sample Daily Checklist

Daily Checklist - Bookkeeper   **Date** _____

Instructions: Keep this checklist on your desk and check off items throughout the day as you complete them.

___ Arrive a few minutes before 9:00 so that you have time to hang up your coat, use the restroom, get coffee, get settled, and start work by 9:00.

___ Check voicemail messages, email, and inbox.

___ Answer the phone between 9:00 and 10:00 and during receptionist's lunch hour. Use a friendly, professional voice: "Good morning, thank you for calling (company name), this is (your name). How may I help you?"

___ Create, update, and refer to your daily to-do list.

___ Keep check register(s) current to ensure daily bank-balance accuracy. Make sure all checks, payroll and payroll tax deductions, and automatic debits are accounted for and entered in QuickBooks. Ask supervisor to transfer funds to/from the line of credit, as appropriate.

___ Create customer invoices daily for completed jobs. (Use Invoicing checklist.)

___ Receive payments daily. (Use Receive Payment checklist.)

___ Keep track of payroll dates and make sure timecards are entered in time for payroll to be processed on time.

___ On payroll days, complete Payroll checklist. (Print out and check off Payroll checklist.)

___ Review and enter vendor invoices daily and ensure that you have correct information for coding and job costing. Consult with appropriate staff as needed. (Use Vendor Invoice checklist.)

___ Prepare for Friday bill-paying on Thursday. Make sure all vendor invoices are entered properly. Print AP aging report from Quick-Books and highlight bills you propose to pay. Give report to CEO for approval.

___ Pay bills on Friday. (Use Bill Paying checklist.)

___ Track collection of funds from clients and follow up as needed to expedite payments. (See Collections checklist.)

___ Take a 10-minute break during your first four hours of work, before lunch, and as close to halfway through your shift as you can.

___ If it's the last week of the month, print out and begin Month End checklist.

___ Punch out for an unpaid half-hour lunch break within five hours of starting today's shift.

___ Take a 10-minute break during your second four hours of work, after lunch, as close to the middle of your shift as possible.

___ Back up QuickBooks each day before leaving.

___ Finish filing before leaving.

___ Every Friday, empty trash and straighten up office.

___ Keep this checklist current and accurate at all times. Get permission from supervisor for any needed changes.

___ Make sure to clock out without incurring overtime, unless it has been approved by your supervisor.

___ Put completed checklist on supervisor's desk at the end of each workday. Print out a new checklist for the next workday and leave at your desk.

___ Before leaving, turn off printer, computer, and copier. Lock file cabinet with checks inside. Turn out lights.

Your Own Daily Checklist

I strongly suggest you make your own daily checklist. Not only will you feel less scattered, but you will be a great role model for your staff. Fewer things will fall through the cracks. You will prioritize more efficiently, and you won't be constantly giving yourself mental reminders to do routine tasks.

As the owner or manager, you have too many things to juggle and remember. Be a good role model and make your life easier by making a checklist for yourself. Your checklist might include a walk-through of the restaurant when you first come in, for example. It will remind you to review the pile of checklists in your inbox. It will remind you to check on your managers at a certain time.

My daily checklist reminds me, in a specific order, to do things such as charge my phone, turn on the ringer, and close my apps. Next item, check both of my voicemails (I write down my passwords here and how to fast-forward, delete, and so on). Then I check my calendars. Then I update my to-do list. Then I check both emails, and so on. The checklist ends by reminding me what I need to pack up in my briefcase before I go out to my clients. When I find myself getting overwhelmed, I turn myself back to my checklist and always make sure it gets done first. Many people make the mistake of fighting fires first, and when they have time, they do their checklist. This is backwards: Do your checklist first, and it will help you prioritize which fires to fight and when.

You will find it is a big weight off of your shoulders if you do these routine things in order at the beginning of the day, before you tackle any projects. It will keep you from feeling constantly scattered and behind. If you use your checklist to make your way through the routine things that must be done before you start on projects, you will feel better the whole day. This is a powerful technique for time management, and many of my clients love it. And by the way, don't hesitate to put personal things on the list—maybe you take a break from your home office every Thursday afternoon to water the plants, for example.

Checklist Skills

Remember that once you have developed your checklists as a tool, you need the skills to administer them properly.

Have your new employees start their checklists on day one. This is important—you must let them know you are a stickler about checklists, and you should enforce this from the very start. Your checklist is a great training tool, so start your new employees by having them check off the things they know how to do. Each day they will check off a few more things, and you'll know how far along they are in their training. Before long, both they and you will have the satisfaction seeing all of the items checked off each day.

Be sure to use the 13-point Checklist Skills list below. These are both *training* and *management* skills.

Checklist Skills List

1. Resist the urge to write your checklists, print them out, put them in a binder, and let them sit on a shelf. First, people will forget to look at them. Second, they will soon get out of date, and if someone *does* look at them, he won't know which parts are correct and which parts are outdated.

2. Have your employees print out their daily checklist every day and keep it on their desk or on a clipboard that they keep near them. In some cases, the file can stay open on the computer desktop and be checked off without being printed.

3. Keep your checklists in an electronic form, such as a Word document. Don't print out a bunch of hard copies that will quickly become obsolete. Add an item to the bottom of the checklist that reminds employees to print out the checklist for the next day and leave it where they will see it. Include the path on the computer so that the person can find the file.

4. Add instructions to the top of the list: "Keep this checklist on your desk/clipboard and check off items each day as you go along." This item is on the sample checklist.

5. Add another item to the bottom of the checklist that reminds the person to put the completed checklist in the supervisor's inbox (or email it to the supervisor) before he leaves. This item is on the sample checklist.

6. Add instructions about breaks and punching in and out at the correct time.

7. Add any little (or big) things that tend to irritate you if they aren't done correctly.

8. Make sure your employee is giving you input if things on the checklist aren't exactly correct—and change them as soon as they need it. Keep the checklist so up to date that if your employee broke his leg and couldn't come to work for a month (this happened to a client), someone else can step in and take over.

9. Make sure your employee turns the checklist in to her team leader every day, and that the team leader reviews it. (The team leader may be you or a middle manager.)

10. Make sure your staff knows that their team leader is actually looking at the checklists to make sure they are completed and the work really was done. People figure it out pretty quickly if no one is reading the checklist.

11. Make sure your manager or team leader is monitoring how his team members use the list. He should have items on his check-list telling him exactly how and when to do this monitoring.

12. If the team leader isn't you, the team leader's checklist should instruct her to collect all her team's checklists for the day, review them, staple them to her checklist, and put them in your inbox. You will have a nice pile of checklists that ensure that your staff is at the very least telling you they have done all of their work.

13. Use your checklists actively to help you manage. If you are having an operational problem, look to your checklists to see what isn't spelled out as it should be. Anytime you are concerned about something being done incorrectly, your first thought should be, "Is it on the checklist correctly?"

Training

If you want your employees to do their job right, you must invest in training! Don't assume they will naturally do things the way you want them to. They aren't mind-readers. Many employers assume that they have hired a clone of themselves and that the employee should have the common sense to do things the same way the owner would. *Au contraire*! The burden is on you to show employees exactly how to do their jobss.

Even if you've hired someone with experience, you have to train them. Many employers think that a new employee will know the best way to do things, just because that person has held the same position at other companies. Often the experienced new-hire will train more easily, but you'll likely have to train him out of bad habits he has developed elsewhere. You should assume that the new employee has a different idea from yours about how to do most tasks. And, you should have ascertained during the interview that he is willing to conform to your way of doing things.

Just how do you train? The easiest way is to use your checklists as your main tool. The time you put into your checklists will pay you back a thousand-fold in reduced training time and in reducing the number of items that will get dropped off the list over time.

If you have everything in line, you will have a daily checklist that, for example, tells a restaurant worker to turn off the grill at 9:00 and clean it at 9:15 using the grill-cleaning checklist. You may only need to *show* the worker how to clean the grill one time, because the steps are written down on the grill-cleaning checklist. You may require the worker to fill out the grill-cleaning checklist the first five times she cleans the grill and staple it to her daily checklist, if the procedure is fairly straightforward and if there aren't any commonly forgotten items. After that, you can assume that she has mastered the technique if the grill looks good when you come in the next day.

This assumes that you are organized enough to remember to check what the grill looks like—or that it's on your manager's checklist to walk around and inspect various things before starting his day. As I mentioned before, owners should have their own daily checklists, reminding them to do routine tasks, such as reviewing their managers' checklists.

As you train, add missing details to your checklist. It takes only a couple of minutes to add a few details or make a few corrections to the checklist.

A word to the wise about training: Any standard you set needs to be maintained by your own management consistency. If you own an ice-cream parlor and you require your staff to weigh a scoop once an hour to make sure the portioning is correct, you need to make sure that's really happening. If this task starts slipping to every two hours, then twice a day, and then once a day, you will find it takes twice as much managerial effort to correct the habit and get it back to the correct frequency than it would if you had stayed on top of it from the beginning. Be wise and keep your standards up from the beginning; it will make your job much easier.

Here are a few things to remember about training a new employee: Create a plan for the training schedule, make sure the employee has a mentor, and don't leave your employee alone on the first few days.

As your company grows, it is wise to develop a training checklist with a training path and training procedures for each position. A training checklist contains all of the items your company requires for training. This might include the orientation program, a tour of the plant, an introduction to a certain set of employees, a training video, and of course the daily checklist. It will include check-ins at regular intervals by the appropriate supervisors. Your manager's checklist will have an item reminding her that when she has a new employee, she must fill out the new-employee checklist, which will of course include a reference to the training checklist.

If your company is large enough and has the resources to be really organized, you can create a training system that includes written study materials, written tests, and training videos. Or better yet, nowadays there are wonderful interactive online training methods that make it interesting for your employees to learn.

An aside here: The general rule should be that the employee begins by learning whatever system you have in place. Once he has mastered that, then he should be encouraged to suggest improvements. If you have an employee who immediately wants to change your system to his, you're in trouble, and you hired the wrong person. It's important to explain this during the interview and again as soon as you begin to train the new hire. Again, the new employee should be required to learn his job completely so that he understands how all of the systems work together before he is encouraged to suggest changes. An employer who lets an employee take time out of his job duties to change things around during training is allowing the employee to divert his energy away from fully learning the other tasks.

Over the years, I have found that employers often believe that they need to tell an employee something only once, and the person will remember it. Long ago, before I started routinely using checklists, I found that I generally had to tell people at least twice and sometimes three times before they would reliably remember sometimes. And even if they remembered the instructions in the first few months of training, the tendency was to forget it or eventually change it around to how they felt like doing it.

This is one reason why checklists are so important. You certainly don't want to be repeating everything two, three, or more times. Even if the item was repeated in your written or video training, the employee may or may not remember it. Let's face it; those materials can be really boring. This brings us back to the reality that if you don't have it written on a checklist, don't expect your employees to remember it, and even more important, don't expect them to keep doing it correctly for a long period of time.

Some employees tend not to ask questions when they should, and they make decisions and judgments they shouldn't. They can be way off on a wasted tangent before you even know it's happening. You have to keep this type of person on a short rope and train her to slow down and ask questions. It's very difficult to get this type of employee to change, so it's much better to weed these people out before you hire them.

And a last word about training: It never ends! New skills will be added to the checklist and job description as new technologies and new company needs emerge. All of your staff members, including you, are in continuous training mode. Use your evaluations as an opportunity to reflect on whether each employee needs to be retrained in some area that has slipped or needs to learn a new skill.

The Promotion Path

Along the same lines as making the pay range and raise policy clear, if you wish to have happy, long-term employees, it is wise to create a promotion path for them. If you have a restaurant, for example, you may start people out as a dishwasher, promote them to a prep cook, then a cashier, then a team leader, then an assistant manager, and then manager. If you are an electrical contractor, you can start out a technician as a helper, promote to an apprentice, then a level 1 electrician, a level 2 electrician, a level 3 electrician, a team leader, and finally a foreman. Each level will have specific skills that the employee must master before he can move to the next level, and each level will have its own pay range. If you have a lot of steps, the pay steps can be quite small. This way, your employees can see how they can move up and improve their pay, their skills, and their value to the company.

I help my clients create a promotion path document that shows all of the levels so that employees have something to aspire to. Some employees reach a certain level and for whatever reason don't progress beyond it. There isn't necessarily anything wrong with this. You can encourage your staff to stretch to the next level, but it's up to them how far they want to reach.

It's possible for this to backfire a little once the employee has over-reached her potential. If you have promoted someone who isn't able to excel at her new position, you will have to figure out what to do at that point—move her back to her old position or sideways to a different department. However, in the big picture, you are better off challenging your staff than letting them get stagnant or bored. Bored people move to another company. Members of Generation Y especially tend to move along if they aren't happy.

Use your promotion path document during your employee evaluation in order to help them set goals and maximize their skills and pay level.

Evaluations

Ah, the dreaded evaluation! If you are organized, have your system set up right, and follow the rules, you can take evaluations out of the dread zone and into the zone of logic. Most employers hate evaluations because they feel they will be pressured for a raise, and they don't know how to decide what's right, and/or because they have been avoiding telling the employee what is wrong. Don't avoid! Be honest! A good evaluation system can help you do that in a matter-of-fact way.

Don't you think it's only fair that you let your employees know what's expected of them and then give them feedback on how they're doing? Don't carry your ideas of what you're looking for around in your head! Again, your employees aren't mind-readers.

And again, with evaluations there are tools and there are skills. The tools are the evaluation form, the raise policy, the promotion path, and the calendar system for scheduling evaluations. The skills are in how to implement these wisely. I will give you instructions for both.

The Evaluation Form

Name _____ **Date** _____
Period Evaluated _____

Using a scale of 1 to 10, rate each category.

Category   **Score**
Comments

Promptness and attendance   _____

_____

Relations with other staff and teamwork   _____

_____

Attitude   _____

_____

Takes directions well   _____

_____

Admits mistakes and learns from them   _____

_____

Judgement   _____

_____

Initiative   _____

_____

Accuracy   _____

_____

Efficiency and deadlines   _____

_____

Job skill level   _____

_____

(Add more of your own categories)

Total (add scores):   _____

Divide by number of items to get average score: _____

Goals:

List goals from previous evaluation. Review each one and make notes here about progress:

_____

_____

_____

_____

_____

_____

_____

_____

_____

_____

_____

_____

New goals:

Make specific goals with dates for completion.

_____

_____

_____

_____

_____

_____

_____

_____

_____

Evaluations are important for a number of reasons. You can see now that they can give you a structure for helping your employees learn, grow, and master their jobs. This will give them a sense of pride and accomplishment, making them more loyal. If you have an employee who doesn't wish to learn, grow, and master her job, you have hired the wrong person. However, some people just move to a certain level and stay there for many years, and there isn't necessarily anything wrong with this. If you push someone beyond her own abilities, you can end up losing a good employee by encouraging her into a role at which she fails.

Evaluation Skills

1. Schedule evaluations based on hire date. Don't try to do them all at the same time.

2. Be on time. Schedule an appointment with your employee at least two weeks in advance of his evaluation date and *do not change or postpone it*. This is unfair to nervous employees, who

may read into you postponing or changing their evaluation or who may be nervously anticipating it. The date you set should be within a day or two of the employee's actual anniversary date.

3. When you schedule the appointment (two weeks ahead), give the employee a copy of the evaluation form to complete and bring to the meeting. (You will fill out your own copy.)

4. The supervisor should complete the form in advance and meet with his supervisor for input a week beforehand—not at the last minute.

5. Don't omit any bad news, and don't inflate the employee's ratings to avoid dealing with something you have put off. No avoidance! It's very awkward to tell an employee who has been there a few years and received good reviews that a portion of his performance has always been substandard but you never bothered to tell him. He has evidence to the contrary in the form of his past evaluations.

6. Decide about the employee's raise after completing the form.

7. There shouldn't be any surprises to the employee. If there are any problems or weaknesses, you should've been working with him all along. However, if there *are* problems, stop and deal with them now! You can apologize for not mentioning it earlier, but this *is* an evaluation after all, so this is the time to bust yourself if you've been avoiding issues.

8. Compare your evaluation ratings to the employee's ratings. Did he rate himself as a 10 on efficiency, and you rated him a 7? This gives you good information to work with. Find out where the disconnect is between your assessment and his.

9. Review each category and discuss what needs improvement and what is already great. Discuss how you rated the employee compared to his self-evaluation scores.

10. Always give at least three examples for each category if performance needs to be improved. If the person's phone demeanor needs improving, for example, first say how it

needs improving and then give examples of what went wrong and when. For example, you might say, "Sometimes you forget to follow our phone script when you answer the phone. When I called in the other day from my cell phone, you forgot to say, "This is Danny, how may I help you?" Then give two other similar examples.

11. Remember that this is a discussion, not a lecture. You will all dread it much less if you can pull that off.

12. Set specific new goals together. For example, a goal might be to improve telephone demeanor from a 7 to a 10. In order for your employee to do this, you will need to tell her exactly how. A brighter voice? A more helpful demeanor? Better enunciation? Never letting the phone go to voicemail? A goal can also be something like learning a new software program or other skill in the next three to six months. Print out your Promotion Path document and review the employee's promotion path opportunities. Write up a specific plan to achieve the new goals and then put it on the supervisor's daily checklist to remember to follow up, and also put it on the employee's daily checklist.

13. Remember, you want A+ employees. That means a score of 8 to 10 in all categories. Use that as a basis for your goals.

14. Use your number rating system as a basis for pay raises. (See the "Pay-Raise Policy" section.)

Pay-Raise Policy

It's extremely important to have a pay-raise policy to go along with your evaluations. If the raise policy and the pay parameters on the job description aren't laid out clearly, the employee will often spend a huge amount of time, energy, and emotional drain trying to judge how big of a raise he can get from the boss, convincing himself he really should be paid much more than he is, and just plain getting up the nerve to approach the boss. Often the employee will talk to other employees, and they can get each other stirred up and indignant that they haven't gotten a raise, or they may feel that they should all get more money instead of the boss getting a new car. A tremendous amount of time, energy, efficiency, and goodwill are lost when these pay issues aren't laid out clearly in advance. Whether or not an employee gets a raise becomes a free-for-all instead of a no-brainer.

One of my clients, the head of a software company, dragged his heels about creating pay-raise policies. Therefore, any time one of the employees got up the nerve, there was a long discussion in the owner's office about why the employee should get a raise. Inevitably, the owner would cave in and give a raise. Word would get around, and each of the other employees would do the same thing. This was very disturbing to the owner, who really didn't want to give raises just then and who didn't have a system for making the right decisions about raises. The amount of productive time spent on employees preparing and making their arguments, getting upset, and then sharing the results with their co-workers was amazing. The whole workplace was in an emotional uproar. You can avoid this by delineating a pay scale on your job descriptions and creating a pay policy (see below).

Sample Pay-Raise Policy

Pay will be reviewed, and pay raises may be given following the employee's annual evaluation review.

Pay raises will be based on the following criteria:

1. The company may provide annual raises of 1–4% based on merit, inflation, and company profitability. All of the following factors must be present for an employee to earn a pay raise intended to help keep up with inflation: merit, actual inflation, and company profits:

   - Employee must have an average evaluation review score of 8 or greater.
   - Employee must have no single score of less than 5.
   - Employee's current pay must be less than the maximum for that job position.
   - Employee must meet all goals set during previous evaluations.
   - Company must have met profitability goals.

2. Merit raises: Employee may be awarded additional merit raises for exceptional performance if all of the above conditions in #1 are met.

Now that you have read this raise policy, you should be able to see that the process of giving a raise will be a straightforward task of reading the policy and following it.

Reports as a Management Tool

Some of my clients initially shrink from the term "reports" and claim that they refuse to get bogged down in red tape. In response, I explain to them that yes, you do want to avoid red tape and excessive reporting. Reports should be quick and concise. If you have the right reports in place, a very few minutes per day spent on a report can make a difference of thousands or tens of thousands of dollars per year to your bottom line.

Many business owners shrug off the fact that their employees extend their paid breaks by five or ten minutes per day. Yet they don't want their staff to spend the same amount of time on creating simple reports that will save tens of thousands of dollars over the year.

Many people have worked for large companies that required reports that seemed meaningless and tiresome. It's your job as an employer to explain to each employee how the items on her report affect the company's overall health and profitability. Then you can explain how a healthy company benefits the employee, with a secure job and steady pay raises when merited. Most employees cannot connect the dots unless you explain it to them.

Reports are an invaluable tool not only for you to get the information you need and want, but to hold the person using the report accountable for results. Each department, even if it consists of only one person, should report its results as often as appropriate. You should always have targets so that the department can measure results. Here are some examples of things you should have your employees report:

- *Salespeople* should compile contacts made, meetings with potential clients, quotes made, and sales.
- *Sales mangers* should report the department's contacts or leads, meetings, quotes, and sales. These should be in a spreadsheet

that calculates contacts per meeting, meetings per quote, sales per quote, contacts per sale, and so on. The report should also track each salesperson's closing ratio and the average ratio for the department. The sales manager should get the average gross profit margin by salesperson from the bookkeeping department.

- *Operations managers or team leaders* for construction or similar industries should compile hours bid compared to hours paid, labor dollars over/under target, and materials over/under target. This should be shown by job, by month, by quarter, and by year.

- *Restaurant managers* should calculate daily, weekly, and monthly labor costs in dollars and percent, compared to target. Restaurant managers should also calculate food-cost percentage monthly compared to target. Over/short should be shown in dollars. Restaurants should also report cash over/short by day, week, and month.

Making your expectations clear by requiring reports and setting targets is the only reliable long-term method for tracking whether your company is staying on track with profitability. It's also crucial if you hope to delegate effectively so that you can work less. Whenever possible, I have my clients create a profit plan, which is a spreadsheet projection for the company's own particular formula for profitability. This creates goals for the company in all categories. The items on your manager's report should be tied to your profit plan goals.

Here is an example of how a report can quickly pay off for you. One of my clients had a bakery and was working seven days a week and losing money. Her labor costs were 30 percent too high. I showed her how to implement a manager's report and hold the production manager responsible for keeping labor to target. We created the report, set targets, and created an incentive for the manager to exceed the target. Within a few months the company was profitable, and within two years the owner was working part time. Please read the full story in Part Three of this book.

Manager's Report	Monday		Tuesday		Wednesday		Thursday		Friday		Sat		Sun		WEEK TOTAL	
	Target	Actual	Target	Actual	Target	Actual	Target	Actual	Target	Actual	Target	Actual	Target	Actual	Target	Actual
Sales $	1200	1136	1600	1681	1600	1436	1700	1756	1900	2026	1900	1895	1500	1549	11400	11479
Over/Short$	1.2	-1 / -1	1.6	-2 / -3	1.6	-2 / -5	1.7	0 / -5	1.9	-2 / -7	1.9	-2 / -9	1.5	4 / -5	11.40	-5
Over/Short%	+or -0.1%	-0.09%	+or -0.1%	-0.12%	+or -0.1%	-0.14%	+or -0.1%	0.00%	+or -0.1%	-0.10%	+or -0.1%	-0.11%	+or -0.1%	0.26%	+or -0.1%	0.18%
Labor %	28.00%	31.25%	28.00%	27.07%	28.00%	31.69%	28.00%	26.48%	28.00%	27.39%	28.00%	29.29%	28.00%	29.37%	28.00%	56.70%
VOID $		26		0		32		12		0		0		0		70
Refund $																
Employee Purch $		50		50		50		50		65		65		55	350	385
Labor $		355		455		455		465		555		555		455	3,214	6509

Instructions: Fill in the green cells only. Each week open the master file and create a new renamed file called Manger's Report week of _____

Note- if you see the #VALUE error, put a zero in the empty cell so there is a number to reference to

Important: Enter an = before you enter a number in a cell

Report Skills

One way to make reports successful is to keep them simple. Have each manager measure three to eight categories that he is responsible for. These might be anything from contracts signed to labor percent to dollars per hour shipped from the fulfillment department. Reports deal with numbers, so whatever you are measuring must be able to be done accurately, in numbers. In general, ratios or percentages are crucial. It's important to know what the labor cost was for the week, but it's even more important to know what it was as a percent of sales.

Always have targets listed on the report, and have the person who is directly responsible for the results fill out the report. The act of filling that number in the blank or in the cell requires the employee to pay attention to it and to consider what needs to be done to improve it. Since the target is right there next to the actual number, it's easy to make sure the employee stays on track.

You must give the person who is responsible for the results *control* over the results. It makes no sense to dictate the labor schedule to the warehouse manager and then hold her responsible for labor as a percent of sales. Your manager must have the ability to adjust her warehouse labor schedule based on sales volume if you are to hold her accountable for results. You may require her to have you okay each change so you don't lose control entirely, but you need to give that person the ability to make the changes needed to get the desired results.

Make your reports due on the same day each day, week, month, quarter, and so on. Always set up a meeting to discuss the report with your managers. Usually a weekly meeting is appropriate for discussing weekly totals, and you can meet monthly to discuss monthly totals.

Incentives

There are three ways to get what you want: goodwill, incentives, and consequences. Incentives and consequences work the same as the carrot and the stick. By far the most effective is goodwill, combined with making your expectations clear. These two things should always be front and center. However, I highly recommend incentives in many situations—particularly those that are measurable and therefore rewardable on a specific mathematical level. The classic example is a sales commission. It's easy to measure, so the industry has made it standard to reward compensation on results. In general, I have found that what works best for sales is part hourly or salaried pay and part incentives.

A general rule is to tie incentives to parts of your operation where you have the most to gain by efficiency. If you are a general contractor and you want your labor costs to come in at or under the bid cost, reward your team leader or foreman by giving back half of the company's savings as a bonus when the cost comes in under bid. This is a little tricky to set up correctly because you should be awarding this not necessarily on individual jobs but on all the jobs combined. And the employee needs to see at least some of the bonus very soon after he earns it, so you need to devise a system that gives a partial bonus for monthly results, a partial bonus for quarterly results, and so on. It's important to capture *all* of the hours, not just the hours someone reportedly said went to the job. And it's also important to have a way to monitor quality so that you don't give out a bonus on a job where the quality suffered due to rushing.

For incentives to work, an employee must be rewarded for something that is specifically under his control. The result you are giving a bonus for can't be too broad or be affected too much by other staff. It doesn't usually work, for example, to reward employees a percentage of the company's gross profit or a percentage of net profit, because there are too many different things that affect a company's profit that are beyond the control of that employee. An employee can work hard to be efficient in some way, but if the owner goes out and buys an expensive company car, it can negate anything the employee has done.

It does work, however, to reward a salesperson a percentage of the gross profit on a large custom job she sells, because she has direct control over negotiations with the customer. It works very well to reward a production team for exceeding their efficiency goal, as long as the goal is clearly communicated and you track the quality. I have found that it works best to give a bonus to the production manager, who then communicates the goal to the team. It generally isn't necessary to give the team members more than a modest reward and plenty of congratulations and camaraderie. People love to be part of a team working together to achieve a goal. To do that, you need to create goodwill, make your expectations clear, measure results, and communicate the results in a very timely manner to the employees.

General-Management Techniques

None of the tools or skills I have discussed will do you much good if you don't have good general-management skills. Your general-management skills are communication techniques that make your staff feel valued, respected, and happy in the workplace. These skills will help you create the goodwill you need from your staff to keep them satisfied and working efficiently on a long-term basis. If they aren't satisfied, they won't stick around. If they aren't efficient, the company won't be profitable, and therefore it won't be viable in the long run.

To use good management techniques, you must make your expectations clear and train fully. Then create feedback loops (checklists, reports, evaluations) so that you and the employees know what they're expected to do and how successful they are at doing it. Check in regularly and let them know what they're doing right and what needs to be fixed or done differently. Start with a tight leash (but don't make it chafe), and let them earn their freedom by proving themselves. When you're confident that their performance is accurate in any given area, give them space. But keep a sharp eye out in case something slips.

Create goodwill by being respectful, being a good role model, being polite and clear, following through with your promises, being consistent, giving feedback, praising when appropriate, being honest, having fun, treating everyone as your "customer," managing each individual according to his needs, and in short being a good human being. We will explore each of these things in the section below.

Make Your Expectations Clear

Remember, for each of these things you have both tools and skills. The tools for making your expectations clear are your organizational chart, job descriptions, promotion path, interlocking checklists, training, evaluations, pay policies, reports, incentives, and your daily communications verbally or by email. The skills for making your expectations clear are all of the things mentioned above.

The Carrot (Incentives), the Stick, and Goodwill

Guess which of these works best? Goodwill works by far the best for most great employees. Incentives work next best, and the stick rarely works very well. So when should you use any of these?

You should use goodwill every hour of every day. This is how you build a loyal, happy staff—once you've hired the right people. I will give you specific examples of how to create goodwill in the next section. The reason you put incentives into the mix is that you want not only a happy staff, but also a productive one and therefore a profitable company.

I have also found that there is an important correlation between a happy staff and a productive staff. If you have a staff with too much time on its hands, that's when you often have the most infighting and dissatisfaction. When people don't have enough to keep themselves busy, they often find time for office politics. And don't take their word for whether or not they are busy or not—only about 10 percent of your staff will really let you know if they don't have enough to do or if they're not being productive. My clients often complain that their employees aren't productive, while at the same time their employees are saying that they have too much to do.

What generally fixes this problem is for the employer to select the correct workload for the staffing level. This is easier said than done. I will give you some real-life examples of how you can deal with this in the next section. I had one client, for example, who had an employee she liked very well but who was wasting time on the job. I had the client solve the problem by simply filling up the employee's inbox. You can read the full story in Part Three.

So you can see that these are two major keys to a happy staff: goodwill and the correct workload. People are happier when they are productive and are pulling together as a team to meet their targets. When a person or team hits a target, they have earned incentives of 1) pride and satisfaction in meeting the target; 2) praise from the team leader, owner, or supervisor; 3) perhaps a fun reward, such as brownies on Friday afternoon; or 4) perhaps a monetary reward if the person is the manager.

When should you use the stick? I hope very rarely, and only with problem employees. First of all, the stick should always be a polite one. Let's face it; an owner is carrying around an implicit stick every minute of the day due to the imbalance of power in the workplace. As an owner in an at-will state, you can terminate someone's employment anytime you wish, and the employee has no control over that. Many business owners forget this. They feel as if they are the ones with no control, because they don't know how to get employees to do what they want. The reality is the reverse. The fact is, you have the power in the relationship, so there is no reason for you to be anything other than polite.

Another implicit stick (and reward) is your employee evaluation. If you have been honest and communicative with your employee, she will know that she stands to get a poor evaluation if you aren't happy with her everyday results. Because of the pay policy, she also knows that she won't be considered for a raise if she doesn't maintain a minimum performance score in all categories. It's your job to remind her of this if her performance is less than excellent. This again is a type of stick. If you really think about it, there is a fine line between a carrot and a stick sometimes. Is the lure of a raise a carrot, or is the threat of not earning a raise a stick?

If you get to the point where you need to write someone up for disciplinary action, it's a form of not-so-subtle stick. If your employee has gotten to this point, most likely either you have hired the wrong person or you have managed the person poorly. Occasionally, someone just has a turn for the worse in his life and inexplicably turns into a problem employee when at one time he was a great employee.

How to Create Goodwill

Always treat your employees with respect and as team members, rather than as people to boss around. Be sure your new hires know you are supporting them all the way. Be available for questions. Check in daily at the beginning by asking new hires whether they have any questions, problems, or concerns. Be encouraging and don't criticize, but *do not* avoid correcting them when they make mistakes! Nip problems in the bud.

Be supportive and noncritical, and make sure all of your employees know you are on their side. This is especially important when you're working with people from Generation Y (born from approximately 1980–1990). Their generation can have a skewed perception of excellence. Many were raised by parents who lavished praise even for a mediocre or poor result. People from Generation Y can be sensitive about being corrected for making mistakes. Be tactful about showing them how to succeed, rather than pointing out mistakes.

If you find you have someone who right off the bat is defensive and whose feelings are hurt when you correct him, you can try explaining to him that he will need to learn to take correction gracefully, but this isn't something that is particularly likely to change. It means you failed to screen well enough for those qualities, and it means you might be wise to let that person go early and find someone who is more secure.

To keep your staff happy for the longest time, it's important that you learn how to change your management style to fit each employee. No two people are exactly the same, and each one needs to be handled a little differently. Some employees feel rejected if you don't check on them or consult with them regularly. Others like to be left alone to do their work. Still others need to see a request in writing before they will take it seriously. Some people want to juggle multiple projects at the same time, and others prefer to take one thing from start to finish. Some people need you to stand up to them when they get a little pushy; others you will have to draw out to make sure they aren't holding back with a problem.

Many general-management principles apply nearly universally. On the other hand, people are different and therefore respond differently to different management styles. Some people love the military top-down style (although most people don't). Some people just need the smallest hint from you to correct their behavior. Others need a direct statement from you to do so.

It helps tremendously to be a student of personalities if you're going to be a manager. In my opinion, it helps you at all levels of life—when relating to your child's principal, being a good parent to your kids, and understanding your friends. When you understand personalities and what motivates people, you can understand how to manage them to their fullest potential. There are many good personality systems: Myers-Briggs, the Enneagram, astrology, and more. My personal favorite is the Enneagram because it's fairly simple, it's accurate, and it helps you understand people's underlying motivations.

Role Modeling

Modeling the behavior you want from your employees is powerful. It's especially important to be a good role model to your middle managers so that they will manage their own employees correctly. By managing them correctly, you will teach them to manage their staff in the same way you are managing them.

Matter-of-Fact Feedback

Learn to praise when appropriate and learn to point out a mistake when appropriate. You must be able to do both of these consistently! You don't have to do these things on the spot, although that is best if you're able to give matter-of-fact feedback when you aren't angry or upset. Important rule: If you're upset about something that happened, wait until you have calmed down before addressing the issue. It can wait. Reflect on what you need to say and how you should say it. Say it in a calm, matter-of-fact way: "I've noticed you were late twice this week. Can you tell me what the problem is?" Then after exploring the cause, "If you're late again, I'll have to write you up. You need to be here a few minutes before your shift so that you have time to take off your coat, use the bathroom, get your coffee, get to your desk, and start working by 9:00."

If you think or know that something has been done incorrectly, start by calmly sitting down with your employee. Point out what you see without being accusing, and ask what's going on. Always give the employee a chance to explain her point of view first. You may find out you were mistaken, that the employee wasn't trained properly, or any number of things you don't expect. Even if the situation is tense, ask the employee to give her point of view first. Really listen to see whether she has a valid point. If not, explain clearly and matter-of-factly what you see and what you expect. Most people don't want to make mistakes, but when they do it's your responsibility to point them out tactfully.

Correct Your Employees in Private

If someone makes a mistake and needs correcting, don't embarrass the person by pointing it out in front of other people. Take him aside in private and communicate the problem in a matter-of-fact, respectful way. However, there are times when you can tactfully correct someone on the job, in front of others. Suppose you're on the job with your roofing crew, and you can see that someone isn't using your preferred technique to cut the materials. You can kindly say, "Let me show you a great way to cut flashing." You can have the rest of the crew gather around at the same time if they also need the same training. This makes it seem less like you are singling anyone out.

Treat Everyone as Your Customer

Everyone is a customer on some level. If you don't treat your customers well, they'll go away. That's obvious. But the same is true with employees and even vendors. If you want a truly good working relationship with your vendors, treat them as partners. You may need a favor someday, and they will be inclined to do it for you if you have excellent relations with them.

The same goes for employees and your employees' families. They are all your customers. If you need to ask your employee a favor—for example, to work on New Year's Day to finish a customer's job—it's not likely that he will say yes if you don't have excellent relations with him.

Be Unfailingly Polite

Be consistently nice to people. Always tell the truth and be straightforward about what you want. Give praise when it's deserved and tell people the truth, respectfully, when they do something wrong. If you have a problem with something, tell your employee, vendor, or customer politely. Never lose your temper—if you get angry, excuse yourself, cool off, and create a strategy to deal with the situation.

Recently, a client told me a story about an incident that happened in the workplace. As the owner, he came across an employee doing artwork while on the job in a clerical position. The owner lost his temper and said something nasty to the employee. The employee quit and sued the company for sexual harassment—she found an unethical attorney to take on a suit with no merit. The business owner's attorney said it would cost at least $25,000 to go to court to prove his innocence. The unethical lawyer offered to settle for $12,000, and the business owner accepted it as the least expensive option in terms of money, time, effort, and stress. I believe the owner made the right decision for his business by settling the case. He is now insured against employee lawsuits, and I suggest you do the same for your business. But the moral of the story is, don't make your employees mad at you, even if you're in the right. The worst employees are usually the ones who are most likely to file lawsuits, but the potential is there for anyone. Even if you must reprimand or fire someone, do it politely!

Here's a tip that works very well to create goodwill. Ask your employees to do what you want as though you were asking a favor. You can foster good relations by saying, "Would you do me a favor and get me this report by 3:00? I really need it for a customer," instead of saying gruffly, "Get me this report by 3:00 and don't be late!" In both cases you have make your expectations clear. In the first case, however, you are asking instead of demanding. The employee understands it's not negotiable; however, she is likely to respond quickly and enthusiastically when asked nicely, instead of waiting until the last minute so that the boss has to sweat a little.

It's very effective to *ask* instead of telling or demanding. If you are specific and always say *what* you want, *when* you want it, and *why* you want it, you will get much better results. Here's another scenario: You slip the work into your employee's box two days ahead of time and assume it will be ready at 3:00 on the day you need it. That's no good— you haven't said when you want it completed.

Along these lines, here's a story about a client who excels in creating goodwill but isn't able to give good, honest feedback. This business owner is unfailingly polite, consistently nice, and has lots of integrity. He is respectful and kind. His employees love working for him so much that he has almost no turnover. The downside is that he isn't good at giving constructive feedback. Employees exhibit the same negative behavior traits year after year. Evaluations are whitewashed, and raises are given even though the employees need to make improvements. Because the owner has high personal standards and is an excellent role model, this has created a mostly good workforce. But the owner has sacrificed excellence by not being willing to work with the employees to help them become their best.

Don't Expect Your Employees to Listen to Your Problems

It's lonely at the top, and you shouldn't expect it to be otherwise. You are the boss, the leader, the role model. If you need a therapist, hire one—but don't expect your staff to be sympathetic about how hard it is to be a boss. Just be very clear about what you expect from them regarding their performance and follow these managment techniques.

The most important thing you can do as a manager is to create goodwill and at the same time make your expectations clear. Following is a story about a business owner who is just naturally a great manager and a master at creating goodwill. Most owners are *not* naturally good managers. However, those who are can create an amazing amount of goodwill and can actually get away without using some of the management tools that most people need. Here is a short story about one of these remarkable people.

Susan: Mortgage Broker

Susan runs a mortgage brokerage. She has a small team of loyal, long-term employees who perform efficiently, willingly, and happily. She takes her time explaining exactly what she expects in every situation. She habitually trains and monitors operations every day. She treats her employees with great personal respect. Because she is secure in the knowledge that she has the power to locate and train people who will provide excellence in the workplace, she can calmly communicate what she wants. Like a good parent, she sets limits and expectations clearly. She also consistently treats her staff politely and points out how important they are to the company. She makes them feel special and valued on a routine basis.

Because Susan is one of those rare people who can naturally manage people, and because she has a small staff, she is able to run a shipshape company while working about 15 hours per week, without using the tools I mentioned, such as evaluations, checklists, incentives, and manager's reports. She is savvy enough to keep a keen eye on potential problems—for example, if an employee is supposed to open the office at 9:00 a.m., Susan occasionally calls at 9:01 to see whether the phone is answered.

Would her life be easier with checklists, job descriptions, evaluations, and employee manuals? Yes, it would. But in her case, they aren't a necessity.

Training and Management Checklist: Tools and Skills

❏ Develop goodwill from day one.

❏ Make sure the employee feels you are in his court.

❏ Create an organizational chart and respect the chain of command.

❏ Invest in training via checklists and hands-on explanation.

❏ Train with daily checklists.

❏ Train with procedural checklists.

❏ Make sure reports are mentioned on the daily checklist— when they are due and how they should be turned in.

❏ Use incentives that work.

❏ Give annual evaluations.

❏ Continue to use your checklists on a daily basis. Continuously update them.

❏ Rely on reports.

❏ Make your expectations clear.

❏ Be consistent. Don't let standards slide—it's harder to get them back to where they should be once standards have been lowered.

❏ Enforce the rule that the employee first learns the system that is already in place. Then the employee can make suggestions and asks for permission to make changes.

❏ Be supportive and available.

❏ Don't avoid telling people what needs correcting.

❏ Learn to praise at the right time and point out problems at the right time.

❏ Give matter-of-fact feedback.

❏ Always be respectful.

❏ Change your management style to fit the person.

- ❏ Keep your chain of command clear.
- ❏ Hold your employees accountable.
- ❏ Create a promotion path.
- ❏ Be a great role model.
- ❏ If an employee isn't working out, stay on top of it and hold him accountable until you need to let him go.
- ❏ Have some fun. You may spend more time with these people than you do with your spouse, so loosen up once a while. But…
- ❏ Don't try to be friends with your employees. And in general, don't hire friends unless you're willing to turn that relationship into a boss/employee relationship.
- ❏ Be a good human being. You can be nice without giving away the farm.
- ❏ Ask, don't demand.
- ❏ When asking for something, be specific about *what* and *when*. Don't forget to give the employee a due date.

Chapter 5

How to Let Someone Go

First of all, you owe it to your employee to have all of the tools and skills that are covered in this book up and running. This is only fair, and it allows your employees to know exactly what is expected and when. If you've waited to implement these things until after your employee has been with you a long time, you owe him a timeline to get his performance in line. Some of these timelines can be very short. For example, if you have someone who is chronically late, you can give him three warnings in the period of a week and then let him go right after that. Or, if the problem is, for example, an accuracy problem, you can use your employee evaluation form and give the person a series of 30-day evaluations to see whether he improves quickly enough to suit you. In any case, you owe it to your employee to make it clear what he needs to change and how quickly it must change.

I often talk to employers who are afraid to let an employee go because they fear some kind of backlash. This is a poor reason for not letting someone go. Maybe you're afraid that other employees' morale will be negatively affected, or that the employee might report you to the labor board or sue you, or that you might not be able to find someone better as a replacement. You might be concerned that the employee will take the customer list and become a competitor, or that the employee will collect unemployment, which is expensive for you. But I have found the main reason why an employer doesn't want to let an employee go is because he doesn't want to be the bad guy.

I tell my clients who are hesitant to let someone go that if the job is a bad fit, they are doing both parties a favor in the long run. An employee who is disliked by her employer is almost never a happy employee. She belongs somewhere she will be happy, and a different employee deserves to get the job so that everyone can be happy.

Regarding the fear that it will be bad for staff morale to let an employee go, it is much worse for morale among your other employees to keep a bad apple on the team. Your staff won't respect you for keeping a poor performer on staff. You're being a co-dependent boss if you let a problem team-member stay. You will start to lose your great employees, who would prefer to work on an excellent team.

When it comes right down to it, you need to be very clear about what you want, give the bad employee three warnings, and if she does not respond, be ready to let her go. When you let someone go, do it when other employees aren't around. Escort the person to her workstation to collect her things, present her with her final check, and do not let her back on the premises unless she has permission. Plan ahead of time to protect computer files and make sure you have passwords and locks changed, if applicable.

Part Three

How It All Fits Together: Case Studies

So how does this all work in real life? I will illustrate the common mistakes that many of my clients make, and I will give you some case histories of success stories. Keep in mind that most of this won't happen overnight, but you can make some dramatic changes within a few days or weeks.

Chapter 6

The Bakery

Tools: incentives and reports

Roberta owned a high-end production bakery. Her company delivered baked goods to several counties, and her products were carried by distributors around the greater Bay Area. When I first met her, she worked seven days a week and slept on the floor in her office several nights a week instead of going home. Her business was unprofitable, but she had a great product with an excellent following of customers. She had a crew of production workers who helped her, but, like the video-store owner mentioned earlier in this book, she ended up picking up all of the loose ends and working 60 or more hours per week. However, by the time she implemented all of my suggestions, not only was the company profitable, but she didn't have to work in production anymore. Roberta went home every night after working an eight-hour day, five days a week. Eventually, she cut back her work time to three hours a day, two days a week—only six or eight hours per week.

The first thing we did was look at her numbers and see that her labor costs were too high by 5 percent of sales. We could see that if we got labor costs to target, Roberta would be making a fair profit. Then she could focus on increasing sales, thereby increasing profits to a very healthy level.

To lower labor costs, we did a fairly simple thing. Roberta had a production manager named Donna. We set up an incentive system whereby Donna would earn a bonus of half the labor dollars saved when the total monthly labor cost was under budget. To do this, we had to have a way to track labor so we could calculate the bonus. We first set up a manager's report. The bookkeeper filled in the weekly sales, and it was Donna's responsibility to fill in each day's labor dollars spent on herself and her crew, and to total up these dollars each week. Then she divided the weekly total by the weekly sales to see whether she was under her 30 percent target. If she was, she could see how many dollars she had earned that week as a bonus, assuming she wasn't over budget the following week. At the end of each month, she received her bonus based on the entire month. It's important to note that Donna knew each day and each week where she was according to her target. Also, note that the final bonus was calculated by the bookkeeper, with real numbers from the accounting system.

When I first visited the production facility, I knew just by looking at the crew that they were exceeding their ideal labor budget due to inefficiency. The employees were moving slowly and without focus or purpose. This was mostly because this was Donna's style. Therefore, a fairly predictable thing happened when Donna was given her labor targets: labor didn't improve! In fact, costs got a little higher. Donna rebelled and complained about the new report, and she refused to fill it out regularly. She swore that it was impossible to meet those targets, and she was angry about the new changes.

The owner did a good job of making her expectations clear, and she gave Donna two warnings that her performance had to improve. Soon Donna quit, leaving the door open for real improvement.

Roberta had an efficient production-team member, Manuel, who was happy to step into the position of production manager. He filled out his manager's report every day. The next time I visited, the employees were focused, purposeful, and moving quickly and efficiently. Within two weeks, Manuel was earning a bonus of approximately $400 per month. His team was united, worked well together, and functioned very smoothly.

Manuel didn't pass any of his bonus earnings along to his team, but he did tell his team when they did or didn't meet their targets. He would sometimes buy them treats to celebrate their success. Over the years, I have found that, counterintuitively, it usually doesn't work as well to split the bonus with the team members. I think there are a few reasons for this. First, it tends to cause bickering about who is getting how much and whether each person is getting her fair share. Second, the amount each person receives gets diluted. And third, the most important motivation for team members working well together is what I have been calling *goodwill*. Good management creates goodwill by making expectations clear, being respectful, and praising when appropriate. Manuel was doing all of these things. Even though he was giving his staff only token rewards, those rewards recognized the team's success. When employees know they are successful, it creates much goodwill on the jobsite.

Now that Manuel was keeping the labor costs down, the company was profitable. The bonus was also tied to product quality and tied to meeting food-cost percentage targets. In other words, if Manuel wanted his bonus, he had to keep product quality high and food costs to target. This way, the product standards were kept high, and at the same time food wasn't being wasted or stolen. Please note that the manager had direct control over all of these items: labor efficiency, product quality, food portioning, waste, spoilage, and theft. Therefore, his bonus was directly tied to his results. As long as the pricing formulas were correct, the manager had control over food costs.

At this point, Roberta had the time to focus on increasing her sales to a point where the company's profits were at the level she desired. We created a marketing plan, and she took on distributors, expanded her routes, and started providing wholesale goods to places like Trader Joe's. The happy ending: plenty of profits and few hours worked in the business.

Chapter 7

The Restaurant

Tools and skills:

- Organizational chart
- Job descriptions with promotion path
- Daily and procedural checklists
- Hiring skills

This next example may seem long and complicated, but the owner got amazing results by sticking with the program and implementing everything I asked him to do. He was so deeply in the hole when I first worked with him that it took him more than two years to turn his company around. It seems quite miraculous to me that he was able to do this, because when I first met him he had run through all of his capital, he wasn't paying himself, he was behind on his payroll taxes, and he was talking to a bankruptcy lawyer. By the time I finished working with him, he was back on payroll, his taxes were paid up, and the company was profitable. Here's how he did it, step by step.

Mike, a restaurant owner, was continually frustrated with the food presentation and the level of service at his restaurant. His business was unprofitable, but he had a very good customer base.

Like the video-store owner mentioned earlier, he was constantly running around telling people to fix things, so he had very little time to do anything else. He was run down, stressed, and unable to take time off because he didn't trust his employees to do the job right. He felt he had to stay until closing so that he could make sure everything was done correctly. He had managers and team leaders in place, but they weren't holding their own teams accountable. In addition, he had a huge turnover because employees didn't like the hectic atmosphere, and because he wasn't hiring the right people. He was spending large amounts of time on hiring and firing.

When we sat down together and looked at his numbers, I could see right away that both his food costs and his labor costs were too high, and that was why he wasn't making a profit.

I knew he wouldn't have the time or energy to address the food and labor costs until he had control over his employees' performance, so we started with checklists.

He had a number of job positions: manager, team leader, server, dishwasher, and so on. I asked him which two positions were causing him the most problems, and we started there with checklists. For the counter checklist, we included tasks such as how the food needed to be presented and how often various areas needed to be checked for cleanliness. We included items such as portioning instructions and how to thank the customer properly. Each time I asked him, "What else isn't being done correctly?" he would come up with a new item to put on the list, until he couldn't think of any more. Certain items were standard for all checklists, such as when to take breaks, how to punch in, and what to do if the checklist needed an update. I gave Mike careful instructions about how to administer the checklists and came back a week later.

What a difference! Mike was no longer complaining about the employees on the floor, because they knew exactly what to do now. But he was complaining about his managers, because they still weren't taking responsibility for their team members' work. Therefore, we spent about half an hour making an organizational chart so the chain of command was clear. Next, we spent a couple of hours making the manager's checklist, which had items such as making sure team members clocked in and out on time, distributing checklists to the team members' clipboards before they arrived, making sure team members were using and checking off their checklists, and other items that specifically told managers how to manage their team members, including how to judge when to send employees home early if business was slow. Again, I left the owner with instructions on how to implement this new batch of checklists and came back a week later.

The next time I visited, a predictable thing happened: Some of the managers and team leaders thrived under the new lists, but one of the managers resisted using the checklists and refused to be held accountable. Predictably, this was the manager with whom the owner had been having the most trouble before the checklists were made. It was time for what we call "positive turnover"—in other words, letting go staff members who aren't willing to do their jobs. We discussed exactly how Mike would handle the dismissal—by giving the manager three written warnings with each warning listing very specific things that needed to change. We identified a team leader who worked under the problem manager and who Mike thought would be a good person to promote.

The next time I checked in with Mike, he had implemented the written warnings and dismissed the manager who still refused to follow the rules. He had promoted the team leader to manager, promoted a floor worker to team leader, and hired a new person at entry level.

By this time Mike had implemented daily checklists for all the positions, and the managers were making sure the checklists were being printed out and checked off by each employee. Although Mike was still stressed about not making money, he wasn't complaining about employee problems anywhere near as much. However, he had as much turnover as before because he wasn't hiring properly. The new-hires who weren't interested in being held accountable were being let go more quickly because the new checklist system held them accountable, and the good employees were staying longer because things were calmer, happier, and more orderly, and they felt pride in doing their jobs well. This was all due to the checklists being administered properly. But the great employees resented the team members who weren't pulling their weight.

So next, we decided to work on how to hire properly. Mike was used to looking at resumes and screening them for restaurant experience. However, he wasn't screening for the *qualities* he was looking for. He didn't bother checking references more than superficially, because he didn't feel the former supervisors would want to disclose much to him, for fear of being sued. He got a glowing reference letter from one employee and then hired her, only to find out that she was a disturbed individual. He later discovered that she had stolen the letterhead and forged her previous boss's signature.

Mike was already ahead of the game because he had his daily checklists made. It took just a few minutes to brainstorm and create a list of the qualities he was looking for in an employee. We used the hiring checklist included in this book to work our way through each item. Next, we created three job descriptions for the three positions with the most turnover: deli worker and prep cook, dishwasher, and cashier. These job descriptions were all about responsibilities rather than the tasks listed on the daily checklist. They included items such as providing the highest level of customer service; keeping the workstations neat, clean, and organized; and following all health laws and policies. Making three of these job descriptions took only an hour or two.

We also put some thought into skills tests. For example, he decided the prep cooks would demonstrate certain tasks, such as measuring, slicing, and chopping, using hand tools and mechanized equipment. The dishwashers weren't required to take a skills test.

One by one, Mike and I went through the items on the hiring checklist in this book. Most of these items only have to be created once, and he could use them repeatedly any time he wanted to hire someone. Some items on the list were skills he would retain, such as how to screen a resume, how to do the phone and email interviews, and most importantly, how to conduct the in-person interview. Mike was in the habit doing most of the talking during the interviews and "selling" the applicant on the job instead of really digging in and seeing whether the applicant was a good fit. He learned how to graciously question each applicant about her future plans, her immediate financial needs, and her likes and dislikes to see whether she would be a good fit.

Mike also stopped hiring the best of any given batch and was willing to wait until a really excellent person who would be a great fit showed up. Over time, Mike built an excellent staff with very low turnover for his industry. Because he was willing to spend some extra time during the hiring process, he saved huge amounts of time and money by reducing turnover.

Once Mike switched over to his new hiring process, he had large blocks of time to work on increasing profitability. This was because his staff had their checklists and knew what was expected of them, and the managers were now taking responsibility for operations instead of Mike continuously putting out fires. He also started training his managers to do most of the hiring tasks, so he only had to sit in on the main interviews.

Now that Mike could focus on profitability, we started analyzing the numbers. I showed him how to generate numbers through his bookkeeping system that would let him set food and labor targets and track them weekly and monthly. Mike was missing his food targets by about 8 percent and his labor targets by about 3 percent, according to restaurant standards. My experience of analyzing thousands of financial statements for various types of industries allows me to put my finger on what is out of line for all types of expenses. The combined 11 percent by which he exceeded his targets amounted to more than $74,000 per year when we added worker's comp and payroll taxes to the labor overage.

Again, because Mike now had the time to focus on these issues, we laid out a fairly complicated but very doable action plan to reduce his expenses. Mike would lower food costs in several ways: by raising prices by 10 percent (a $6 item now sold for $6.59, and the customers never commented on the increase); by correcting over-portioning and adding procedures to the checklists to keep portioning correct; by monitoring and taking inventory of valuable foods, wine, and beer to lower theft; and by setting a weekly budget for food purchases.

Mike learned to correct labor costs by multiplying expected sales each week by the labor target and then creating a staffing schedule for that dollar amount. This was then monitored each week by special reports we put into place. By the end of the process, we were able to get labor costs 2 percent under budget and food costs 2 percent over budget, which averaged out to our overall food and labor budget.

Mike's style of restaurant required relatively low labor compared to other types of restaurants, but his food costs were fairly high because he wished to keep fairly large portions. These two items, as I mentioned, canceled each other out, so he was able to meet his overall food and labor budget.

Mike now felt that his employees were for the most part happy and performing well, and turnover was much lower. He didn't have to babysit his employees on every little item anymore. His monthly profitability had increased so that he could take home a salary of more than $6,000 per month for a thriving but moderate-sized restaurant. He was now ready to implement even more tools to ensure longer-term, loyal staff. Now it was time to implement employee evaluations, a promotion path, an organizational chart, incentives, and daily reports.

We started on daily and weekly reports, in order to help each shift manager be aware of various targets and because restaurants are especially vulnerable to theft of cash. Like many restaurants, Mike had not installed expensive software to track sales, over-rings, refunds, food costs, employee time tracking, and so on. But even so, an overall manager's report was important to track the data and results.

The manager's report tracked daily, weekly, and monthly sales, labor costs, over-rings, refunds, cash overages/shortages, and food costs. Each of these items was calculated as a percent of sales. The manager filled out the report daily and did weekly and monthly calculations as well. He knew what the target was for each. For example, the labor-cost target was 28 percent, the food-cost target was 32 percent, and the cash overages/shortages target was 0.10 percent. Because the manager or shift managers were filling out the report, they were essentially holding themselves accountable for the results. Mike reviewed the numbers daily and had a brief meeting with the manager weekly to stay on top of things. If any of the numbers were out of line, Mike would immediately get involved to help the manager troubleshoot.

Now that we had accurate reporting, Mike could regularly monitor his business to make sure it stayed profitable. And because he had his checklists in place and good hiring practices, he could trust his employees. The result was peace of mind along with his new profitability.

Chapter 8

The Plumbing Company

Tools: all items on the hiring checklist

Frank owned a reputable plumbing company with a team of excellent plumbers. He grew to the point where he needed help in the office. One day, a bookkeeper who had formerly been a plumber at a different company walked into Frank's office and asked for a bookkeeping job. Busy and desperate for help, Frank hired him on the spot.

Frank's new bookkeeper turned out to be unsatisfactory. He was unreliable, moody, and prone to drug use. But Frank had to have someone in the office to take care of things while he was out in the field. And he didn't know how to go about finding someone who would be a good employee until I introduced him to the tools on the hiring checklist.

Frank was smart enough and patient enough to tackle every item on the hiring checklist with my help. We created every document we would need in the correct order. When it came time to place the ad, Frank asked me to screen the resumes for him, do phone interviews, and then send him the ones I recommended. Even though the job market was flooded with applicants, I posted the ad twice to get three excellent candidates. Frank interviewed all three, and one was a perfect fit. She was happy to have the procedural checklists to work from. She has an extremely pleasant personality and is excellent with all aspects of her complex job duties. To this day, Frank and his employee are a perfect match and are very happy working together.

Chapter 9

The Retail Store

Tools: all of the correct hiring tools
Skills: screening skills and interview skills

Robert owned a retail store and had a staff with high turnover. He was a very nice person who treated his employees with respect. He had all of the tools from the hiring checklist in place. Yet, he still hired employees who just didn't fit what he was looking for.

I took a look at his most recent hire, David, who was unhappy in the job. I looked over David's resume and noticed that for years he had been working as an office temp for various jobs through a temp agency. He did have some ongoing part-time work in retail, but that was his only retail experience. When I spoke to David, he said he loved temp work because as soon as he mastered each job and started to get bored, he was able to move on to a new position. His eyes really lit up when he described this process of mastering a new position and then moving on to a new challenge. I asked him why he had applied for a permanent full-time retail job, and he said he liked the store and liked Robert, and he thought he would be happy there. When I talked to him even more and asked him what else he really liked to do, he got very animated when he spoke of the DJ business he ran on the side. He said he was unhappy that the weekend retail-store hours conflicted with his DJ business. David was clearly not a good fit for this job!

Often employees are unrealistic about what will work for them, especially when their biggest concern is to get a steady paycheck coming in. A good interviewer could almost certainly have discovered this same information from David during the interview. Perhaps his enthusiasm for the temp and DJ jobs would have been a bit more reserved, but a good interviewer would have thought to ask David which hours are most popular for a DJ and would have noticed that these hours conflicted with the store hours. A good interviewer also would have seen all those years of temp jobs and would have asked David what he liked about temping. A red flag would have gone up. And to take it a step further, if the resume had been screened better, the preponderance of temp jobs and the lack of strong retail experience would have been noticed, and David never would've been invited for the interview in the first place.

My next step was to sit in on an interview with Robert and an applicant. Robert talked most of the time and was content with short answers from the applicant. When he did ask a question, it was a leading one. Robert came up with what he thought were clever questions, but he was really just avoiding what he really needed to find out. He mostly talked about how great his company was and how nice it was to work there.

These are very common mistakes! I have done hundreds of interviews, and it's surprising how often I have helped the applicant come to the conclusion that the job doesn't fit what he really wants. As soon as I see some kind of inconsistency between what the applicant wants and what the position calls for, I point it out right away and ask the applicant to comment. If I think the applicant is just giving lip service by saying the conflict doesn't exist, I pass him by. If I'm not sure, I strongly urge the applicant to do some soul-searching to make sure this potential conflict can be worked around. I explain that I don't want him to take the job if he's going to want to leave pretty soon due to this or any other issue.

The moral of the story is that the owner had all of the tools in place, but his skills were lacking. This led to a workplace with high turnover.

Chapter 10

The Printing Company

Tools: organizational chart, job descriptions, checklists, and evaluations
Skills: management skills

Aileen was the owner of a thriving printing business. She was able to attract excellent employees and excellent customers. She produced a superior product and had loyal customers.

Her problem was that she was working 10-hour days tending to the intricacies of a complicated production system. She was constantly frustrated by the loose ends that her employees left to her. Her health was beginning to suffer due to the stress.

Aileen was astute and ready to make the needed changes. I worked with her to successfully implement an org chart, job descriptions, checklists, and evaluations. Once she used these tools in addition to learning good management skills, Aileen's stress levels decreased hugely. She was able to come to work late in the morning and leave early when she wished. She could schedule manicures and club workouts during the daytime, and she had time to focus on marketing to grow her business even more. She weeded out clients that were not profitable and bought her own commercial building. Her business became so profitable that it became quite a project to invest all of her profits into real estate, stocks, bonds, and other investments. She sold her business before she turned 60 and now lives a very comfortable retirement, waiting for her first grandchild.

In situations like Aileen's, I generally implement the daily checklists first. This takes care of the myriad items that tend to fall through the cracks and drive the owner crazy. However, in this situation we first spent about half an hour creating an organizational chart. We did this first because Aileen had several middle managers, and we needed to establish a clear chain of command. It was also an opportunity to coach Aileen about holding the manger responsible when she saw an employee on any team who needed to be corrected. Aileen had been telling all of the employees what to do, instead of holding the manager responsible. When she saw a problem and corrected a team employee, her manager was unaware that there had been a problem. Therefore, the manager didn't have a chance to correct it. Aileen was undermining her managers by going around them to their employees. I explained to Aileen that she needed to hold her managers responsible for all of her team members, instead of managing them herself. You can see how this would lighten Aileen's load immeasurably.

Once we had the roles designated and Aileen understood how they would work, we created each manager's daily checklist. We started with the production department, which was causing Aileen the most stress. Since production was fast-paced and the production line had to be flexible depending on which jobs had all of the elements needed to go to press, Aileen created a series of brief meetings throughout the day during which various managers met to discuss production status. Each meeting was set for a specific time and lasted about five minutes. The time for each of these meetings was on the appropriate manager's daily checklist. Each checklist, you will remember, has its items listed in chronological order. The employee works her way down the list and this way has reminders of what to do at specific times.

The production manager's checklist included making sure all items were ready for UPS by the normal pickup time. It also included items describing exactly when to stop production to start cleanup and what exactly the staff needed to do for cleanup and to close up for the day.

You will also recall that each checklist includes an item making the user responsible for keeping the checklist up to date. The production manager's checklist included an equipment-maintenance item, which reminded the manager to check the maintenance schedule every Monday to see whether he needed to schedule maintenance time for the following week.

All of the managers' checklists instructed them on how and when to check up on their team workers' performance, including making sure breaks were taken at the right time and for the right length of time. Aileen had about 30 employees, so an extra five minutes per day on unpaid breaks would cost her about $8,000 per year, including worker's comp and payroll taxes. The checklist also included an item reminding the manager that overtime wasn't allowed unless approved by Aileen. This was because Aileen was having a problem with overtime showing up on timecards.

I mentioned earlier that I have seen a frightening number of employers turned in to the Labor Board over various labor-law infractions. In Aileen's case, she had been allowing her employees to take their break at the very end of their shift. In other words, instead of taking their 10-minute break near the middle of their shift, they left 10 minutes early but got paid for the ten minutes. Aileen let her staff do this because they wanted to, and she thought she was creating goodwill by doing so. However, a disgruntled employee complained to the Labor Board, and she got audited. The only problem the audit turned up was the break issue, which is technically illegal. Aileen had to spend more than $15,000 in lawyer's fees and a fine. Therefore, in the future she was careful to include exact instructions on the managers' checklists to make sure the employees took their breaks.

Since then, California state law has been interpreted a bit more liberally. However, the point is that you can make sure your staff is following whichever laws or regulations you need to be careful about. And if you have it in writing, on a manager's checklist, it is much harder for an employee to make a legal case against you. But the very best way to avoid legal issues is to hire excellent employees and create goodwill with them by managing them well. Over the years, I have noticed time after time that the employees who cause the most harm are those who are poor at job performance. You can avoid these employees by having good hiring practices, thus protecting you from unnecessary grief and money loss.

Once the production manager's daily checklist was in place, we created the daily checklists for the other managers. Each list included the daily meetings at specific times with the other managers. Soon, at the end of the day Aileen was receiving checklists from each manager in her inbox.

Implementing the checklists is a skill that Aileen picked up well. It doesn't work to hand a checklist to the manager and tell her to fill it out. You must explain the checklist in advance, and the employee who will be using it should be a part of developing the list in order to give her buy-in.

Once the list was ready to go, Aileen set a formal implementation date. On the morning of that day, Aileen made sure that the manager had printed out the checklist and had it on his clipboard. She reminded him to keep the clipboard with him and check off each item. At least once an hour she looked at the checklist to see whether he was checking off items. She asked him to make notes about things that needed to be added or changed and collaborated with him to see how it was working. Aileen was careful to check her inbox that evening to see whether the manager had turned in the checklist. After the production manager had left, she took the checklist and walked around the production area to see whether each item had been completed. She looked to see whether he had printed out the next day's blank checklist, put it on his clipboard, and left it on his desk so he would remember to use it in the morning.

The next morning, Aileen checked in first thing to make sure her manager was using his list right off the bat. She checked in at least twice more that day to see whether he was still using it. Each day, she checked on him less frequently until she was confident that he was remembering to use it correctly. This worked so well that she was ready to move forward and add more checklists for the other managers.

Within a few weeks, Aileen had all of her managers using their checklists.

Chapter 11

The Food Manufacturer

Tools: incentives and promotion path
Skills: general-management skills

I received a call for help from two business owners who were about to go bankrupt. They produced a perishable specialty food item that was distributed around Northern California. The owners were an intelligent, highly educated, and capable couple, each of whom had been successful in corporate America. They decided to quit the corporate rat race and purchase their own company so they could relax and work less. To their great surprise, running a small business was infinitely more difficult than being an expert in their own corporate niches. They had mortgaged all of their properties, had taken out a bank loan, and were about to default on everything.

The first thing I did was set them up on my proprietary version of a week-to-week cash-flow schedule, which I call a payment schedule. They were able to master this in order to juggle their cash-flow problems, and because of this they succeeded in staving off bankruptcy.

The next step was to create my proprietary version of an accrual projection, which I call a profit plan. By creating the profit plan, they were able to see what they had to do to make a profit and pull themselves out of the financial hole they had created. They could also see how long it would take them to do it. It is psychologically important for anyone in this position to know this.

To make a profit, they needed to lower their labor and food costs. To make a *significant* profit, they would have to do both of those things and also increase sales by about 10 percent.

The first task was to determine what the pricing for the product should be, based on the food costs. We determined that food wasn't being wasted, over-portioned, or stolen to any significant degree. Because we knew the cost of the food (due to good bookkeeping), we ran a simple formula to calculate how much we needed to increase prices. The owners had been afraid to increase prices even though food costs constantly increased. They got up the courage to raise prices, and they experienced no loss in units sold. This gave them the confidence to raise prices once or twice every year (depending on how fast costs increased). Thus, they were able to keep up with inflation and keep food costs on target.

Because labor costs are calculated as a percent of sales, it was important to get the correct pricing in place first. We then set a labor target of 30 percent and multiplied that by total sales to get the total labor budget. This was translated into a weekly budget and used to create the employees' work schedule.

The production manager was resistant to the new labor budget, even though he had been involved in the reasoning behind it, as well as the creation of the new schedule. Before this, his employees hadn't been keeping the production facility up to standards under his leadership. He continually came in over budget, even though he had been offered a monetary incentive to come in under budget. He complained that he was underpaid, but he didn't do what it took to make more money by exceeding his targets. He soon left the company and started up a competitor company, which folded within a couple of years.

The owners took the opportunity to promote a production-team member to production manager. This manager was able to meet the labor targets and occasionally come in under budget to earn a bonus. The bonus system was the same one described in the bakery example in this book.

At this point the company was meeting its food and labor targets, paying its bills, and meeting all of its debt obligations. It was time to increase sales.

The food was distributed daily, and the day-old food had to be rotated out by the delivery drivers. They were fortunate enough to have a sophisticated computer program that could track the amounts delivered and rotated back each day. The discarded food had to be kept to a minimum, without the product running out, in order to make a profit. The delivery drivers were held accountable for keeping the correct ratios of discards. The drivers were also considered the sales force.

We set up an incentive system with a flat hourly fee plus a percentage for commissions. A delivery driver with average sales and returns would make about the same as she did before the change. A driver who excelled could make more money, and a driver who did poorly couldn't make enough money to be content. The goal was to keep improving the delivery team until most of the drivers were excellent and making good money.

This system required constant monitoring by the owners and drivers. Each driver was responsible for recording his daily numbers so he could see how he was doing. The owners met with each driver at least once a week and reviewed the numbers. The drivers were responsible for calling on new stores within their routes in order to increase sales and their own commission. Fortunately, the owner who managed the drivers had been a human resources manager in her corporate job, so she did an excellent job of treating her staff respectfully, coaching them, setting targets, and showing them how to maximize their paychecks.

Now that food and labor costs were in line and sales were up, the owners could focus on paying back their debt and improving the production staff. They set up a promotion path in production, starting with Production Team Member Level One, Production Team Member Level Two, and Production Team Member Level Three. Next was Team Leader, then Assistant Production Manager, then Production Manager. Level One had a wage range starting at minimum wage and ending at minimum plus a dollar. This position required the employee to do unskilled-labor tasks, such as cleaning and packaging. There was a list of tasks that the Level One employee had to master in order to move to Level Two. The tasks needed to be mastered at a specific level of efficiency, quality, and skill that was required to move to the next level. This meant that each worker had something to strive for, and they knew what the monetary reward was when they reached the next level. Level Two included some of the same tasks as Level One, but at a higher skill level and higher efficiency.

You will note that there were five levels on the promotion path, in a company with only 15 production workers. This is a healthy structure. One thing it accomplishes is that all of the workers are cross-trained by the time they reach the upper levels. It also establishes a solid backup structure if an employee is sick or leaves the company. For example, if the assistant manager is unavailable, both the team leader and the manager can cover. If the manager leaves, the assistant manager can be promoted to manager, and the team leader can be promoted to assistant manager. If the company has to run two shifts at certain times of the year, the assistant manager can run one shift, the manager can run another, and each one will still have a team leader.

Another benefit of this structure is that the owner is able to see where each employee tops out in abilities. For example, some employees may never make the effort to learn English, even if that is a requirement for the team leader position. Other employees may not have the personality required to manage others, but this may not be evident until they are promoted to team leader. Generally, the employer will want to have several team leaders, one for each shift. The weaker ones will be paired with the strong assistant manager and manager.

One of the basic ideas in this structure is delegation. The smartest managers and team leaders understand that the more responsibility they can delegate to their team members, the better the shift will run. This is because people with a good work ethic feel proud to be trusted with responsibility. If each person takes responsibility, instead of the manager constantly telling people what to do and then picking up the pieces of what was left undone, the team will run like a well-oiled machine.

The production manager did a good job of sharing the labor targets and the ensuing results with the entire production staff. They all knew that if they got production finished by their time-target, they would get acknowledgement from their manager, assistant manager, and team leader. Once the new manager was in place, the entire team pulled together to meet the targets. The production manager didn't share her bonus with the entire crew; however, she did reward them all with a pizza every Friday afternoon if they came in under budget. The employees loved it, and they shared their reward with a feeling of success as a team.

By this time the two owners were profitable, they had increased sales, and they had a solid production and delivery staff with a promotion path and incentives in place. This was such a far cry from when I first met them, when they were on the verge of bankruptcy. They were focused but tired from all of the hard work of turning the business around, but the stress and satisfaction levels were vastly improved. The owners decided it was time to retire and really take a rest. I assisted them in putting together a sales package and advised them on how to approach potential buyers. Within a year, they had found a large corporation to acquire the business for millions of dollars. They hosted a happy thank-you and farewell party for their lead employees and me, and then moved to a beautiful coastal region of California and thrived.

Chapter 12

The Hardware Wholesaler

Skills: assigning the correct workload and pay scales

My client was a wholesaler who packed and shipped large volumes of hardware all over the country. His sales volume was over a million dollars per year, he had a wonderful customer base, and his company did a great job with customer service and accurate packing and shipping. However, he was losing money. I assisted him in identifying the problems and making the needed changes, and within a year he was profitable.

The owner was extremely adept at creating goodwill because he was a truly kind and considerate person. However, he lacked the ability to tell his employees what they needed to correct. Since he was an intelligent, caring, conscientious worker, he was an excellent role model for these particular qualities. The result was an extremely loyal staff of mixed-quality employees. Some were excellent, some mediocre, and some poor. They were all treated as family, and because their bad habits weren't corrected, they were reinforced.

In addition, the company was overstaffed, so the employees had extra time on their hands for bad politics. Squabbles were common. This company was a mixed bag in terms of employee quality and workplace politics. It also wasn't profitable due to overstaffing and salaries that were above the going rate.

The owner refused to fire or lay off staff, which reinforced the problems. However, because of consulting with me, he knew he was overstaffed and that his employees were overpaid.

Just a note here about "overpaid" employees: There is nothing inherently wrong with paying people a good wage—in fact, I am a supporter of the "living wage" concept. However, wages are one of the largest expenses for most companies. Even if they are only a few percent higher than they should be, it can make the difference between profitability and loss. What dictates that few percent? Competition. Competition drives the efficiency model of all companies. If this wholesaler's competitor pays the same prices for hardware as his competition, but he pays significantly less in labor costs, the competitor can sell the product at a lower price. When our generous wholesaler lowers the price to match the competitor, he cannot make a profit due to his higher wages. It's as simple as that. This means that everyone has to meet the efficiency rate and pay rate of the most efficient competitor if they want to make a profit.

Okay, so back to the generous employer. Here is how this scenario played out. Luckily, the company was able to open up new channels of distribution to increase sales significantly. I counseled him not to increase staffing as his sales levels increased. This increased the efficiency and profitability of the company. I also advised him to freeze pay at the current levels. Luckily, the economy was strong in those days, and prevailing wages rose quickly in the next few years. He was no longer overpaying his staff, and they were working more efficiently. Voilà, he was making money!

Chapter 13

The Tile Store and Printer

Skills: assigning the correct workload

Ron owned a tile store, and he had a secretary who was unproductive. She used office time to spend personal time on the Internet, she took overly long breaks, and Ron was left to finish the rest of her work each day. Ron was another "good guy" who was unable to effectively communicate to his employee that she needed to be more productive. I asked Ron if the secretary knew that she was leaving things undone each day. He didn't have a daily checklist, so I guessed that the employee simply didn't have enough work that she knew needed to be done. I instructed Ron to fill his secretary's inbox with a little more work than he thought she could get done each day. His secretary immediately became productive. The long breaks and Internet surfing stopped. She was cheerful and motivated. Her work stayed at the same high-quality level that it had been before. Ron hadn't said a word to her—he just gave her the right amount of work.

I want to emphasize that this is a very common problem (although less so if the country is in a deep recession, when many employers have cut back to the bone due to necessity). However, I still see it commonly during hard times. I had another client who had three people in a prepress department. He discovered that one of them was running an

Internet business on the side, during company time, so he fired the man. This left two people in the department, and it ran fine. Next, the manager of the department moved away, leaving only one person. That person got along fine with the help of a part-time person. At no time had any of these employees indicated that the department was overstaffed or that they didn't have enough to do. The quality of the work didn't suffer when the workload went up; the department was simply overstaffed for years.

I have seen this same story repeated many times over the years with various clients. It's difficult for business owners to know how to staff their positions. This is why checklists are important tools. You can measure the time each task should take and calculate literally how many hours the position requires per week. If you under-calculate, you can always increase staff, but if you over-calculate it's hard to know whether you have wasted money on extra labor.

Chapter 14

Conclusion

Over the years I have seen hundreds of business owners rise to the occasion and turn their businesses around. Instead of laboring under stress, they run a smooth, productive, profitable business. Any business owner who is willing to learn and become proficient in the tools and skills I have discussed has a great opportunity to create a happy, productive business environment.

For More Information

If you would like more information or to request customized help with your business, you may contact the author Annabel Ayres at:

Ayres & Associates
P.O. Box 11224
Santa Rosa, CA 95401
www.AyresNow.com
707-585-3669

www.ingramcontent.com/pod-product-compliance
Lightning Source LLC
Chambersburg PA
CBHW020208200326
41521CB00005BA/295